FROOME

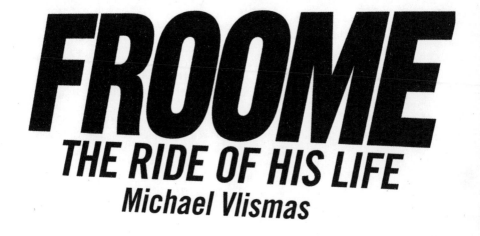

FROOME
THE RIDE OF HIS LIFE
Michael Vlismas

Jonathan Ball Publishers

Johannesburg & Cape Town

First published in 2013 by
JONATHAN BALL PUBLISHERS
a division of Media24 Limited
P O Box 33977
Jeppestown
2043

Paperbook ISBN 978-1-86842-604-1
ebook ISBN 978-1-86842-605-8

Cover by Michiel Botha, Cape Town
Design, colour section and typesetting by Michelle Staples
Set in 12.5/16.5 pt Corporate A
Printed and bound by Paarl Media

Twitter: www.twitter.com/JonathanBallPub
Facebook: www.facebook.com/pages/Jonathan-Ball-Publishers/298034457992
Blog: http://jonathanball.bookslive.co.za/

Contents

Climbing the mountain

Chris Froome @chrisfroome   16 July 2013
Almost went over your head @albertocontador.
Little more care next time?

It is the silence that is the most frightening.

At the end of a gruelling 221 kilometres during stage 15 of the Tour de France, the peloton is dead quiet. No talking. No shouting of orders. No jokes. Each rider has only one thought in his mind. It's right there, rising up before him: the 'Beast of Provence', Mont Ventoux, a meeting point of fact, folklore and pure cycling hell.

Chris Froome had ridden Ventoux before during training, but he had never raced on it in the Tour de France. Yet he was fully aware of the mountain's fearsome reputation.

Its sheer geology is enough to instil fear. Italian Renaissance poet and scholar Petrarch referred to Mont Ventoux as a 'steep and almost inaccessible mass of stony soil'. In a letter describing his own ascent of Ventoux on foot in 1336, Petrarch wrote: 'I rejoiced in my progress, mourned my weaknesses, and commiserated the universal instability of human conduct.'

This legendary mountain in the south of France is by no means a thing of beauty. It has a lunar quality – a mass of bare limestone that shines so white in the baking sun it appears as if it's permanently covered in snow. Its summit is devoid of vegetation. There is no life here and, to make matters worse, for 240 days of the year it is buffeted by the mistral wind, which has its origin in the Bay of Biscay and gathers speed as it whips down the Rhône Valley, eventually reaching its peak strength in this area of Provence, sometimes gusting to 310 kilometres an hour. It is from this wind that the mountain derives its name – Ventoux has its origins in the French *venteux,* meaning 'windy'.

Mont Ventoux is one of the epic climbs of the Tour de France. The other mountains undeniably have their challenges. Alpe d'Huez comes armed with its 21 infamous hairpin bends. The Col du Tourmalet features as the mountain that has made the most appearances since the beginning of the tour over a century ago. Then there is the Col d'Aubisque, a mountain pass in the Pyrenees, and the Col du Galibier in the Dauphiné Alps. All have their special place of honour in the gallery of great climbs in the Tour de France. But, for the tour cyclists, Ventoux is the nemesis. It presents 20.8 kilometres of torturous climbing that demands and takes everything from winners and losers alike.

And there is nothing glamorous or romantic about Ventoux. The average gradient of the climb is 7.43 per cent. The first 5 kilometres are a gradual climb; then, for the next kilometres, the gradient rears up to 9.5 per cent; and for a 2-kilometre stretch, it becomes as severe as 10.5 per cent. Add the pounding mistral and the oppressive heat of over 40 °C, and Ventoux becomes the monster it is in the cycling world.

Chris Froome may not be a devout student of cycling's history in the way that sportsmen like Roger Federer and Tiger Woods have combined their dominance of their games with an almost encyclopaedic knowledge of the eras that have come before them. Froome admits he does not dwell on the past. It's very likely that by not fully immersing himself in the history of Ventoux – or of the Tour de France as a whole – Froome guarded against being overwhelmed by such challenging sections of the tour. For if anything is able to instil fear at the mere thought of it, it is Ventoux.

In his book *Mountain Kings*, cycling writer Giles Belbin refers to Ventoux as the 'bad-tempered, smouldering older brother' of the picture-postcard mountain climbs the tour is famous for. To some extent, Ventoux could be likened to the Eiger in Switzerland – not the highest mountain in the world by any means, nor on a scale with Everest in terms of popularity, but a killer in its own right.

And Ventoux has taken lives. It made its debut as a mountain climb in the 1951 tour, but gained its notoriety in 1967. During that tour, the mountain claimed the life of British cyclist Tom Simpson, who was considered one of Britain's most successful cyclists when he took to the slopes of Ventoux in July that year. He was the first British rider to wear the yellow jersey, which he gained in the 1962 tour. In 1965 Simpson was crowned world champion. But what happened on Ventoux has divided the cycling world as to its opinion of the smiling son of a coal miner from northern England.

Simpson had appeared to be riding well with the lead group, but one of his teammates observed casually that he seemed to be taking on more fluids than usual. Just over 3 kilometres from the summit of Ventoux, during what was then stage 13 of the tour, eyewitnesses recalled how Simpson began weaving across the road before he eventually fell. The British team car was close at hand, and legend has it that Simpson, rasping and out of breath, ordered them to 'put me back on my bike'. Which they did – but the grainy, black-and-white video footage shows him as a forlorn figure, lying slumped over his handlebars. His team tried to push him on. He fell again, and appeared lifeless as they tried to revive him, his eyes staring blankly at the heavens. The official tour medic, Dr Pierre Dumas, immediately had him transferred by police helicopter to the nearest hospital. Simpson died there later that evening. It was only the third death since the tour had begun in 1903 – but it was the most controversial at that point. A post-mortem revealed that Simpson had died of heart failure as a result of dehydration, and alcohol and amphetamine consumption. Pills were found in Simpson's pocket.

A biography published in 2003, *Put Me Back on My Bike: In Search of Tom Simpson*, by William Fotheringham, reveals how Simpson had been afflicted with diarrhoea during that tour and had slipped to seventh overall. He was under pressure from his team to make it into the top five – or lose out financially. The tour's rules prohibited Simpson's team car from handing him water during the race, and he was forced to rehydrate with whatever he could get from roadside bars, including Coke and cognac.

Simpson's death was the first public doping scandal of the Tour de France. But it was by no means the first time drugs had been used in the event. Far from it: since the start of the competition in 1903, riders had consumed anything from alcohol to ether to push their bodies beyond the normal limits of human endurance. And, even before then, cycling had long been plagued by doping. In the early years of the tour, riders openly admitted using whatever cocktail of drugs and alcohol they felt could help them win. Perhaps the only reason Lance Armstrong's case has so captured the world's attention is the openly aggressive way he went about doping and people's sustained belief that he was doing nothing wrong.

Simpson's death drew the subculture of doping into the public domain and prompted the first official drug controls in professional cycling. And he remains an anti-hero of the tour – cyclists either pay tribute to his monument on Mont Ventoux as they ride by or spit on it. Britain's Bradley Wiggins, winner of the 2012 Tour de France, said he always felt a natural allegiance to Simpson: 'For me, climbing the Ventoux is the equivalent of climbing the steps at Wembley Stadium for all English footballers ...' As Wiggins prepared for a stage up Ventoux in the 2009 Tour de France, he told UK daily *The Independent*, 'Tom will be watching over me on the Ventoux. For me, racing up there to try and get on the podium is a kind of homage to him. I don't think enough is made of Tom, and for me going up there on the Ventoux to try and get on the podium when he was the last Englishman to try to do so helps keep the legend alive.' For that stage, Wiggins even attached a photo of Simpson to his bike frame.

The mountain hit the headlines again in the 1970 tour. The great Belgian cyclist Eddy Merckx – at the time, the first rider in history to have won a stage on Ventoux while wearing the yellow jersey – showed that even he was human after summiting Ventoux. 'Le Cannibale', as he was known, had to be administered oxygen after winning this stage en route to an overall victory in the Tour de France that year. 'You know when you are in the peloton and you come near the Ventoux – nobody's speaking any more, you can hear a fly, because it's always very quiet because everybody's afraid about the Ventoux, because it's a hard climb,' Merckx once told Australia's ABC News.

In his book *Tomorrow, We Ride*, French cyclist Jean Bobet, brother of the three-time Tour de France winner Louison Bobet, and an accomplished professional cyclist in his own right, recalls the mood in the peloton when they reached the foot of Mont Ventoux in the 1955 tour: 'It's very hot. I'm going to hell. Not a word. Nothing is more impressive than a silent peloton. Nobody says a word, nobody laughs. Lifting your head slightly, you can make out the shape in the distance, through the mist, of the Ventoux ... You can smell the fear of the men going to a lingering death.'

Louison Bobet won the tour that year thanks to his monumental efforts on Ventoux. But, again, the mountain had cast a shadow over the tour. Frenchman Jean Malléjac collapsed unconscious on its slopes; Swiss cyclist Ferdinand Kübler suffered the same complications; and Luxembourg's enigmatic Charly Gaul had to be treated for stomach ailments. All of these cases prompted suspicions of doping, but the allegations were never proved.

Jean-Paul Vespini, a veteran cycling journalist who has covered the tour since 1990, said of Mont Ventoux that 'to race over the bare summit of the mountain in a heatwave is to defy death itself'.

During the 2013 Tour de France, *VeloNews* cycling correspondent Dan Seaton wrote: 'Success on the Ventoux comes at a steep price: everything you have in you. But the mountain asks the same of those who come up short.'

* * *

In the unlikely event that Froome did not know the full scope of what he was up against on the Ventoux, he had enough people around him who did, and to remind him of the challenge. Speaking to reporters ahead of stage 15, for example, Danish rider Jakob Fuglsang described what lay ahead: 'Sunday is the longest stage of the tour and I think it's the longest finishing climb also, so I think it's going to be a tough stage ... After all the flat kilometres, to hit a climb like that in the final, it will be a day that some guys will experience that their legs don't work the way they used to or the way they expect them to, and just the pure fatigue from a long stage will be important too.'

And now, as the lead bunch sped towards the base of Ventoux, with his Sky teammates having done an excellent job of matching the incredible pace of 47 kilometres an hour set by the Movistar Team to try to crack the peloton, Froome prepared to throw himself headlong into the climb that would define his tour, his career and his life. The British boy from Africa who had learnt his trade riding up mountains in Kenya was about to face one of cycling's ultimate mountains. If Ventoux were to take from him everything, then Froome was ready to leave everything on the side of that mountain.

Sky's Richie Porte and Pete Kennaugh kept up a merciless pace, and they soon caught the last of the nine-man breakaway that had formed earlier in the stage, reeling in Frenchman Sylvain Chavanel at the foot of the mountain. The eccentric Slovakian Peter Sagan brought a short-lived distraction to the task that lay ahead when he pulled his trademark wheelie just before the mountain, and saluted as the peloton charged into battle.

Having placed their man in the perfect position at the start of the climb, Froome's lead group began to thin out at a rapid pace. Porte took over the attack. Alberto Contador, Froome's greatest rival in this tour, and a man also bred for the climbs in cycling, was still keeping pace. But, when Porte glanced back at him, Froome knew it was his cue. With 7 kilometres left, Froome pushed hard, leaving Contador floundering behind him. The severity of the attack on Contador was heightened by the fact that Froome didn't even leave his saddle. Contador, the man who in 2009 had tamed Ventoux on his way to tour glory, and once considered among the greatest climbers in cycling before his career was tainted when he was found guilty of doping, could only watch as the young man from Africa did what Contador's legs and mind no longer could. Perhaps Contador had suspected this was coming ever since Froome had beaten him in the Tour of Oman in February before the Tour de France.

'I came to this tour to win, but Chris Froome is too strong,' Contador told reporters after the stage. 'Froome is superior to everyone else in the mountains. He showed it in the Pyrenees, and he showed it again today.'

As he powered forward, gritting his teeth, Froome was hurting. But he knew that the others were hurting too. 'So much of that sort of attacking is done on feeling; I can feel when it is personally hurting, hopefully other guys are also hurting too. It's mental warfare,' Froome told *The Independent.*

The young Colombian Nairo Quintana still posed a significant challenge to Froome, however. Quintana surged to the front. But so swift was Froome's attack on Contador that he was soon alongside the Colombian. 'He was talking to me, telling me that we should keep pushing to leave Contador behind, that he'd let me win the stage,' Quintana told reporters. 'But I knew it wasn't true, because I knew how strong he was.'

Froome hadn't planned to win the stage. He was more interested in building up a significant time lead over the general-classification riders. The general classification in multi-stage bicycle races tracks the overall times for riders over all the stages. A rider may win one particular stage but still be far behind in the overall standings. For Froome, Quintana was the perfect partner to help him increase his time over the general classification. But, with 1.3 kilometres left to the finish, something moved within Froome. It may have been Quintana's faltering. It may have been Froome's own increased desire to conquer this mountain. 'In the last two kilometres [Quintana] lost a bit of time and I did my maximum to get as big an advantage as possible,' Froome said afterwards.

And with a powerful turn of the pedals, Froome dropped Quintana. Appropriately, but unplanned, it happened near

Simpson's memorial. 'I could tell Froome was stronger than me. I'm not at his level, and I could understand what he did, I knew I wouldn't be able to attack him again. When he went, I went full gas but I couldn't follow his wheel,' Quintana said.

Chris Froome rode to a historic stage win in 59 minutes. It wasn't the fastest-ever ascent of Ventoux on a bicycle. That record belongs to Basque cyclist Iban Mayo, who did it in 51:51 in 2004 in the annual Critérium du Dauphiné Libéré road race.

But Froome's performance on Mont Ventoux was nevertheless significant statistically in many other respects. It made him only the second wearer of the yellow jersey to have won a tour stage on Ventoux – after Merckx had last pulled it off in 1970. He was also the first Briton to have won a stage on Ventoux. And Froome had opened up a lead of 4 minutes and 14 seconds over his rivals. But Ventoux always exacts a price and, like Merckx before him, Froome had to have his lungs filled with what he had left trailing in the mountain air – oxygen. 'I felt faint and quite short of breath. I can't remember taking oxygen before,' he said of the oxygen intervention he needed after the race – for the first time in his career.

Greg LeMond, American three-time winner of the tour, watched Froome's amazing climb and told French TV afterwards: 'It's over. When you're as good as Froome in the mountains, you drop everyone else and there is little they can do.'

It was Froome's greatest day, and it all but cemented his hold on the yellow jersey going into the final week of the

2013 tour. 'I think every cyclist would dream about winning a stage like today. This climb is so historic. It means so much to this race, especially being the 100th edition,' Froome told television reporters.

The *Yorkshire Post*, the mouthpiece of Leeds, the town where Chris Froome will begin his defence of the yellow jersey in the 2014 Tour de France, was among the media that hailed Froome's achievements. 'Not so long ago, the thought of a British cyclist powering his way to the top of Mont Ventoux seemed so fanciful that it was almost laughable,' wrote Nick Westby. 'Time often lends better perspective on events. Just as Tom Simpson's death on Ventoux 46 years ago still sends a chill up the spine of British cycling enthusiasts, so as the years pass, Froome's astonishing ride will be given higher regard. It was a "where were you when" moment for British cycling ...'

But the controversial recent history of cycling means that great performances in the tour are immediately viewed with suspicion. So the following day, what should have been a rest day for Froome turned into yet another grilling by reporters on the subject of doping. 'I just think it's quite sad that we're sitting here the day after the biggest victory of my life talking about doping,' Froome told reporters in a counter-attack perhaps more poignant than any he delivered on the slopes of Ventoux. 'Quite frankly ... my teammates and I have spent months away from home, slept at high altitude on volcanoes to get ready for this race ... training together, just working our arses off. And here I am, sitting here being accused of being a cheat and a liar. That's just not cool. It's been a long battle to get where I am now.'

2

Out of Africa

Chris Froome @chrisfroome   4 July 2013
Haven't changed much over the last 25 years
have I? #throwbackthursday http://instagram.
com/p/bW8LR0mxs3/

(Tweeted at the start of stage 6 of the 2013 Tour de France, with a boyhood
photograph of Froome.)

'Of course I can run.'

That's the standard answer from most young Kenyans when the question is asked. When the BBC ran a survey asking why Kenyans dominate marathons, one of the answers came from Kenyan Elijah Maanzo, who said, 'As young Kenyans, we ran 5 kilometres to school every morning. And as children, we saw our parents run to work. We ran to church, to the river, everywhere. To a Kenyan, running is part of our daily lifestyle.'

Since the 1960s, Kenyans have dominated long-distance running internationally. The rudimentary running track in Iten, in Kenya's Rift Valley, has produced more world champions than any other track on the planet.

But, in a nation where babies seem to be born on their

feet, finding a top Kenyan cyclist would appear to be a far harder task. In Kenya, as in most parts of Africa, a bicycle is a mode of transport. Your legs are what carry you to athletic glory, not a bicycle, for goodness' sake.

But, slowly, newspaper and magazine articles began to filter through about young Kenyans who had a passion for cycling. In these articles, people began to reason that if Kenyans are such great endurance athletes in running, imagine what they could do on a bicycle.

In 2012 John Franklin Hay was part of Bike Kenya, a group of nine friends who cycled almost 1 000 kilometres through Kenya to raise $40 000 to build a school in the north-west of the country. Their route took them into the Rift Valley, the region that has taken on mythical proportions for its ability to produce world-class endurance athletes. Hay wrote in his blog:

As we pedaled toward Narok, we passed this young man, whose name we learned was Joseph. Joseph caught up with us and started riding with us – he on this heavy, single-speed bike and we on our lightweight, multi-speed bikes. When he was still keeping up with us and hanging around after more than 16 kilometres at our 29 km/h pace, we were not only impressed, but concerned. Wouldn't his parents wonder where he was? Did he know what he was doing? Were we putting him at risk? One of our hosts talked with him in Swahili and discovered that he was going to the next town for his family and that such rides were common for him. Wow! I hope the Kenyan cycling organizations find out about Joseph. Actually, we found numerous young men riding these heavy, single-speed bicycles who were able to ride with us at our pace for miles, and frequently up some substantial hills.

But it was a photographer from Singapore who made some of the biggest headlines when he started his project of creating a Kenyan cycling team that he hoped would one day be able to compete in the Tour de France.

Nicholas Leong was passionate about cycling, and captivated by the Tour de France. He also reasoned that Kenyan athletes with such amazing endurance potential should, by rights, also have the potential to become great cyclists. The Jamaicans had done it with their bobsleigh team for the 1988 Winter Olympics, so why not a Kenyan cycling team?

In 2006 Leong flew to Nairobi and then travelled by bus to Eldoret, in the Great Rift Valley. Together with Iten, Eldoret is the cradle of Kenyan distance running and has for decades produced the world's top distance athletes. Why this may be the case has led scientists to speculate about everything from the topography of the region to the locals' gene structure, the altitude (2 400 metres above sea level), the water quality and the socio-economic circumstances that mean Kenyans are predisposed to enduring hardship and discomfort. There has even been a religious theme behind the success of these great men on legs. Irish Catholic missionary Brother Colm O'Connell became the new 'patron saint of athletics' for his role in helping to train a host of world champions since he came to Iten in 1976 to teach geography and save souls.

The Great Rift Valley is a world of myth, wonder and awe in endurance sport. It is a geological trench that runs from north to south through Kenya, a region that has produced some of the greatest endurance athletes the world has ever seen. As leading South African sports scientist Professor Tim Noakes has observed, 'approximately 72 per cent of the most successful runners come from the Rift Valley, which contains only 20 per cent of the Kenyan population'.

Professor Bengt Saltin, a Scandinavian physiologist, has also studied the Kenyan runners and concluded that 'there are definitely some genes that are special here [in Kenya]'.

But could they be genes suited to cycling as well?

Leong set about achieving his dream of creating a Kenyan cycling team, gathering promising riders and acclimatising them to better equipment. In 2008 he put them to the test. Leong took two of his riders to the Alpe d'Huez, one of the most prominent climbs in the Tour de France and an ascent stage most cyclists in the tour dream of conquering. The two cyclists competed in their own time trials on the mountain, which they both finished in just over 40 minutes. The world's top cyclists do the climb in under 40 minutes. Although a couple of minutes can represent a chasm of a difference at the elite level of professional cycling, Leong's experiment was still a tantalising taste of what could be achieved given better equipment and training.

'The Kenyans are coming' was how the cycling media started to portray the country's new sporting focus. But there was one Kenyan who was already making his own impact in world cycling: a dreadlocked man with a radiant smile, who had ridden for Kenya in the Commonwealth Games and competed in Africa, Asia and Australia, and who was on the brink of breaking through in Europe. Much like Leong,

David Kinjah had his own vision for Kenyan cycling. And he would eventually help to shape Africa's most successful cyclist to date in Chris Froome.

Kinjah and the skinny white boy

'Chris's mother asked me if I could teach him, even if it was just how to fix punctures.'

In the village of Mai-ai-hii, north of Nairobi, 40-year-old Kenyan cyclist David Kinjah is surrounded by the laughter of children as we speak on the phone shortly after the 2013 Tour de France. A television documentary shows his shack with bicycles propped up against it. One clothes line has cycling jerseys hanging on it to dry; from another are suspended several helmets. You can hear wheels spinning in the background as bikes are tinkered with and tuned. The scene is far removed from the elite cycling environment of Europe, with its bicycle technicians, crack teams of sports therapists, managers, nutritionists – the arsenal of people whose job it is to forge and hone the elite cyclists of today. Yet this village of tin shacks has given cycling its latest star. And as a result, Kinjah has become a part of the world's cycling heritage. Amateur cyclists from around the world travel to his village for the chance to ride with this gregarious man.

Kinjah opened up the world of cycling to Chris Froome – he was the man who taught Froome everything he knew about bicycles and cycling. And it began with a very simple lesson: how to fix a puncture.

Froome's mother, Jane, was the daughter of a coffee farmer who had emigrated from England to Kenya. His father, Clive, left the UK to run a travel business in Kenya. Here he met Jane and they married and had three sons, Jonathan, Jeremy and Chris. Froome's two elder brothers were educated at the prestigious Rugby School in Warwickshire and went on to qualify as chartered accountants. But his parents split up when Chris was still young. His father relocated to Johannesburg, while Chris remained with his mother in Nairobi.

When Chris was 12, his mother took him to a cycle race that Kinjah had organised. Her son was mad about cycling, she told Kinjah. So please could he just show him a couple of things about bicycles, to entertain him, she asked.

Froome's childhood was not an easy one after his parents split up. Money was tight, and the need to make some sacrifices no doubt steeled him for the rigorous discipline he would later require to become one of the world's top cyclists. But he was cushioned by the love of his mother, and he was blessed with a childhood of pure freedom in the natural world around him. A childhood that was the ultimate adventure for any boy in a country where you might be chased by a hippo while fishing, or shoot stones at one with a catapult from the banks of the river.

Chris and his mother lived at the back of a large homestead in a wealthy suburb of Nairobi. He would try to make some extra cash selling avocados by the side of the road to the wealthy residents of the neighbourhood, joining countless other Kenyan children doing the same for their families. Although a loving and very supportive mother, Jane was struggling to balance the demands of building up her physiotherapy practice and the needs of a boy who had a boundless energy about him.

'It was not easy for them. His mother moved around a lot and she said she didn't want to just lock him in the yard at home all day while she worked,' recalls Kinjah as we discuss those early days in Froome's life.

So his mother and his brother Jeremy put some money together and bought Chris something they thought might help to use up that extra energy – a little BMX bike. Froome loved his first bicycle and it soon became part of his daily life. Then Jane heard about the bicycle race.

'His mother told me that he was very interested in his little bike and she just wanted him to see what the race was about, because we didn't have any space for kids. I think she just wanted to find something for Chris to put his amazing energy into. She asked me if I could teach him, even if it was just how to fix his own punctures. I had this passion to share. It just felt right. And I had my own cycling dreams as well, so I understood.'

An act of fate that seems to suggest Kinjah and Froome were almost destined to become friends is the similar way in which they both started their cycling careers. Kinjah was born in Eldoret, the town known for producing top runners, but his family moved to Mombasa when he was young. Kinjah got into the swing of this tourist coastal town, and beach football began to appeal to him. He joined a group of boys who would gather at the nearest beach and play football for money, gambling on the outcome of the matches. 'That's how we made money. I also started to get very fit that way.'

Kinjah soon realised that if he could get to the beach every day, it would be more lucrative for him. But living 17 kilometres away from the beach made that difficult. So he scoured the local scrapyards until he found his transport – a little BMX bicycle. The same kind of bicycle a young Chris Froome would arrive with in Kinjah's village years later, and that would spark a friendship between the two that has remained close even as Froome has moved around the world following his own career.

Kinjah soon became hooked on cycling and graduated to a road bike. In 1994 he began to take cycling seriously, and his racing took him to competitions in Africa, Asia and Australia. But, like most cyclists, it was to Europe that Kinjah was pedalling. In 2002 his dream came true when he became the first black African cyclist to sign for a European team, when he joined the Italian outfit Index-Alexia Alluminio. The team had just won the 2002 Giro d'Italia (Italy's national pro cycling race), and Kinjah joined them at the end of the year on a two-year contract.

But the fallout from the terrorist attacks on the World Trade Center in the US in 2001 was still busy settling over Europe. Kinjah explains:

The European economy was in trouble and teams were closing down all over the place. The UCI [Union Cycliste Internationale – the governing body of world cycling] came up with a new set of rules to protect the riders and their salaries. We were a Division 1 team, but the new rules stated teams had to present a full year's budget. Most teams worked from quarter to quarter. My boss couldn't come up with the sponsors for a full budget, so the UCI issued him with a Division 2 licence. That meant he had to cut the team by six riders. I was still kept in the team, but we lost sponsors and money became a big issue. Eventually the team just broke up.

One of those who benefited from the break-up was Jan Ullrich, a former German cyclist. Ullrich had his own team, Team Coast, which also folded at that time. One of the sponsors behind Kinjah's team was Italian bike manufacturer Bianchi, the oldest bike company in the world. In 2003 Bianchi decided to form its own team built around Ullrich. It was supposed to be a combination of the two teams that made up Index-Alexia Alluminio and Team Coast. But Ullrich had his own riders, and his focus was solely on the Tour de France. So Team Bianchi was created for him and the Tour de France that year.

The 2003 Tour de France saw Ullrich push self-confessed doper Lance Armstrong all the way, before the American finally claimed his fifth tour victory, with the German finishing second. But Ullrich would eventually succumb to the same doping controversies as Armstrong. Ullrich, the gold medallist at the 2000 Olympics, was found guilty of doping following his ignominious retirement from professional cycling in 2007.

'He nearly kicked Armstrong's butt in the 2003 tour, but I think he had a big dose of EPO [the illegal performance-enhancing drug erythropoietin] in him,' says Kinjah, laughing, still able to see the funny side of someone coming just short of fulfilling his own dream.

After the break-up of his team, Kinjah moved to Belgium for a while where he took part in a few criteriums (circuit races) and then worked in the Netherlands. The friendship he had built up with Froome continued in emails and on the phone whenever possible, and they kept in touch to the day Kinjah returned to Kenya later in 2003. He came home to discover that the young cyclist he had met in his village was now the Kenyan junior champion.

Ultimately, Kinjah's greatest triumph as a cyclist would be his ability to share his passion with the young riders of Kenya – riders such as Froome, and children from the nearby villages who were inspired by this dreadlocked man who showed them you could achieve anything you wanted on a bicycle.

Kinjah's home in the village had become the main base for the Safari Simbaz, the name given to his cycling club. Through Simbaz, Kinjah created a vehicle to share his experience and passion for cycling, and give young Kenyans the means to become either cyclists, bike mechanics or bicycle tour guides, helping them to find their niche in an industry that could give them opportunity and hope. In a documentary that Kenyan filmmaker Mũchiri Njenga called *Our World is Round*, produced about Kinjah's work with young Kenyan cyclists, Kinjah says: 'As an individual, you could only win so many races, but by inspiring others, the opportunities are endless. Cycling transformed my life, and I really wanted to help transform somebody else's life.'

One of the many young cyclists in the Safari Simbaz summed up the hope Kinjah gave him when he said, 'Where my parents could not take me, the bike has taken me.'

Kinjah also communicated his passion to Froome, as well as his experience and a belief that the best equipment does not necessarily make for the best rider. The same lessons he teaches children today are those he taught a young Froome during their time together in the 1990s. 'When you see a father trying to teach his kid how to ride a bicycle, it's because the kid is interested. But, on the other hand, the father cannot wait to see his kid riding the bicycle all by himself.'

* * *

And so Jane Froome drove her son to the little village outside Nairobi, where Chris Froome would become known as the 'skinny white boy' who loved cycling as much as the other boys did. Froome became one of them, easily slotting into the rhythms of daily village life. For the European media that later revelled in this part of his life, it seemed anathema that a white boy could mingle so easily with blacks. But it is hardly uncommon in Africa, especially in a rural environment.

Yet while Chris was happy to spend as much time in the cyclist's village as he could, his mother had reservations. 'When Chris's mom asked me to teach him,' says Kinjah, 'I told her that it would be best if she brought him to my village. When she came to drop him off, she wasn't too sure about leaving him there with me. But it never bothered Chris. After just a few weeks, it was like he'd been living in the village his whole life. He was very much at home and didn't care what the village looked like.'

Kinjah included Froome in everything he did with his bicycles, whether it was going on rides or fixing them. The intimate knowledge Froome gained of bicycles and how to repair them would later mean he would trust few people to do the job for him. That special task fell to South African mechanic Gary Blem for the 2013 Tour de France. Blem is considered one of the best in the business, and has overseen the bicycles of German sprint legend Erik Zabel, British superstar Mark Cavendish and the 2012 Tour de France winner, Bradley Wiggins. And he too received his education at the hands of a black man by the name of Matthews Leganyane, who first introduced Blem to the world of bicycle repairs when he worked at Bruce Reyneke Cycles in Pretoria. It was Blem who, during the 2013 Tour de France, would remind Froome that while he was a British citizen, his roots were in Africa. So Blem put a sticker of an assegai on Froome's bike.

As Froome's knowledge of and passion for cycling grew in his early teens, his mother began to take an interest in cycling as well. 'She started organising these camping rides for us,' says Kinjah. 'She loved the bush and being outdoors, and Chris liked it as well. He loved the freedom of nature. So we started doing more mountain-bike riding.'

During these off-road bike outings through the Kenyan bush – with everything from elephants to the occasional lion in their path – Kinjah started to notice an incredible drive in Froome. Jane Froome noticed it as well, and it concerned her. 'His mom was starting to get worried. She kept saying to me, "Kinjah, you're pushing Chris too hard. He's just a *kijana* [Swahili for young boy], remember. Don't push him too hard." And I'd say to her, "Well, you'll have to help me because he's unstoppable."'

Kinjah remembers one particular ride where Froome's incredible determination showed itself. 'He had come back from South Africa for the school holidays. His mom organised a camping trip to a village with some Maasai friends of hers. It was about 130 kilometres away. My plan was for Chris and me to ride about halfway, and then she would pick Chris up in the car and take him the rest of the way. We started cycling, and when we reached halfway, we stopped so he could get into the car.'

But the young Froome refused. Kinjah recalls how both he and Jane stood there in the bush pleading with Froome to get into the car. The boy burst into tears and refused. 'He said he wanted to do the whole ride with me. So we carried on. When we were about 5 kilometres from the campsite, Chris started riding harder and faster. I could see then that there was something not normal about this guy. When we reached the camp, he was finished. He'd hit the wall, and he had no sugar left in his body. But he'd finished the ride and that was all he cared about.'

Yet Kinjah admits there was still no inkling in his mind at that stage that Froome could ever become something as a cyclist, never mind a Tour de France champion. 'We just had fun in those days. I didn't see him as Tour de France material. It wasn't even in our minds. We were living for the moment then and never thought of the future.'

But Froome was clearly driven towards something more than just a boyhood fascination with bikes. He began pushing himself harder and harder during races. He may not have shared the same genes that made the Kenyans such incredible endurance athletes, but Chris Froome brought something else to the Kenyan equation – a single-minded focus that appeared hidden from the world under the veneer of a humble, almost shy boy. Such was his determination to push himself to the limits that there were times when he would pass out from the exertion of his races and end up in hospital.

Kinjah recalls how, later, when Chris was at school in South Africa, his father would phone Jane from South Africa in a panic, telling of another occasion when Chris had passed out from exertion. Then Jane would contact Kinjah, who had developed an almost parental influence over Chris. 'Please talk to him, Kinjah. Tell him to slow down,' she pleaded with him.

Clive Froome was also concerned that his son's focus on cycling was distracting him from the more serious pursuit of his studies. Kinjah did his best to placate both parents by sending emails to Froome asking how he was doing. 'He would respond by saying things like, "Kinjah, I'm fine. I'm eating more vegetables now for my training." He was learning all the time and getting smarter about his training.'

While Kinjah was increasingly impressed with Froome's dedication and his pursuit of excellence, he still never believed it would take him to any great heights – largely because he considered himself a far better rider than Froome, and he didn't even count himself as Tour de France potential.

But, on top of his protégé's obvious determination, Kinjah saw something else that would later serve Froome well in the high-pressure environment of the Tour de France: the patience of a man who was meticulous, almost insistent, about doing things his own way and happy to wait for a result that may have come faster somebody else's way.

'Chris has always been a very patient young man. He's learnt how to be very patient, even under pressure. You wouldn't see Chris ever getting angry with anybody. Whenever he was frustrated, he would turn it on himself. He would never blame anybody else.'

Froome's perceived shyness is more likely to be just his introverted nature, which in itself has made for the perfect marriage with a sport that demands hours of self-sacrifice and discipline. His success in Team Sky is attributed to the fact that, once he is in agreement with his team managers about the path they are on, Froome follows instructions to the letter.

And while he may have been a quiet type at school, he was by no means shy to the extent of being frightened of the world around him. On one occasion when he was at St John's College in Johannesburg, he phoned Kinjah and they both had a laugh about how Froome was dating two girls at the same time, until he realised they were friends.

'But lots of people don't understand him,' says Kinjah. And at times, not even Kinjah does. He thinks back to when he gave Froome his first pair of cycling shoes. In 2009 Froome handed them back to Kinjah. He told him he could afford his own pair now. That's not what surprised Kinjah, though. It was the fact that the shoes were still in excellent condition, despite years of use. 'He really looked after them. That is how Chris is. He takes nothing for granted.'

Like all competitive cyclists, Froome has also always had a fascination for the colourful jerseys worn by the various race leaders. Early in his career in Kenya, he became aware that the champion riders of each country wear a special jersey consisting of their national colours. So Froome phoned the Kenya Cycling Federation and asked when the Kenyan National Championships were taking place. He was told there wasn't a championship. 'So how do I get to wear the national champion's jersey?' he asked. The person on the other end of the line laughed, then added, 'If you design the jersey and sew it together yourself, you can be the national champion.' And that's exactly what Froome did.

In this vein, Kinjah gave Froome another significant gift. 'A friend of mine gave me a yellow jersey that he had bought in an African market. I gave it to Chris while he was learning and training with me. He was so impressed. He couldn't believe I had something like this and would give it to him.'

In his shack, with the sound of bicycle wheels still spinning in the background and children laughing, Kinjah adds, 'I'm really happy he's got his own yellow jersey now.'

3

South Africa:
A cyclist's education

Chris Froome @chrisfroome   4 July 2013
Incredible day for African cycling, a Saffa in
yellow! Congrats @darylimpey & kudos to
@simongerrans for setting it up #TDF

(Tweeted after stage 6 of the Tour de France, when South African Daryl Impey
became the first African to wear the yellow jersey.)

For someone who is defined by elevation and the amazing
climbs he pulls off on a bicycle, Froome's move from
Nairobi to Bloemfontein to begin his high-school career was
a bigger comedown for him than just the 300-metre altitude
difference between the two cities.

Although Nairobi is a major city, Froome enjoyed the freedom any boy would have loved as he was able to revel in the
natural world around him, and enjoy the community spirit
in Kinjah's village.

Froome's father, a safari tour operator, had moved to South
Africa from Kenya in 1995 to begin a new business venture.
South Africa was opening up under its new democracy.
Mandela was ushering the country back onto the world

stage, in a shining example of a peaceful transition of power never before seen in Africa. There was newfound potential in the country, and Clive Froome felt his son could also benefit from it. So both parents made the decision that Chris's high-school education should be in South Africa, where he would have access to better schools than in Kenya.

'At that stage, we weren't very well off and couldn't really afford to send Chris to a school in Britain,' Clive told *Beeld* newspaper. 'So Jane and I agreed that Chris should complete secondary school in South Africa because the schools were so much better. When his mother later passed away, Chris stayed on in South Africa with me.'

Arriving in Bloemfontein in 1999 when he was 14, Froome found himself in a completely different environment – a predominantly Afrikaans culture in the heart of the farming community of the Free State. Bloemfontein is a far cry from the cultural melting pot of Nairobi, a loud, vibrant capital infused with the cultural spirit of Europe mixed with the throbbing beat of Africa. Bloemfontein is Afrikaner cultural heartland, a conservative town built around the Cheetahs rugby team and known for one of South Africa's greatest boys' high schools, Grey College, which has consistently produced some of the country's finest sportsmen for generations, from Springbok rugby nationals to cricket heroes and Olympic gold medallists.

It would have been fitting for Froome to have found himself in Grey's hallowed halls. Yet for reasons not explained, his parents chose to send him to St Andrew's as a boarder. His first taste of life there in South Africa was not a happy experience for the young Froome. 'It wasn't necessarily an easy school to adjust to and there were challenges,' Clive Froome told *Beeld*.

The teaching staff at St Andrew's have only vague recollections of Froome – largely because of the very short time he spent there. 'Chris was only with us for about six months,' explains John Bridger, deputy headmaster at St Andrew's.

So it was decided that Chris should move closer to his father in Johannesburg. He found himself in the office of Roger Cameron, the headmaster at St John's College for boys, in the plush suburb of Houghton. With its illustrious list of alumni, including some national sports stars, renowned academics and businessmen, St John's helped Froome truly come into his own.

'I remember his first interview with me. He'd come to us from Bloemfontein and there was some unhappiness there. My first impression of him was that of a lovely, well-mannered boy,' says Cameron.

Although his teachers portrayed Froome as one of the quieter boys, this never detracted from his likeable personality. He was actively involved in school life and is described as a solid student. 'He was very much liked by his friends and was popular. But we had no idea what his potential was. Academically, he was by no means top of the pile. But he passed well, and I think he did get some distinctions for mathematics in matric. But while he didn't shine as a top student, he wasn't in trouble academically,' explains Cameron.

Froome's future as a world-class athlete also seemed to remain a slow-burning fire within him and didn't show itself at St John's in the traditional manner of a sporting child prodigy. 'Chris was clearly passionate about cycling, but he also played rugby and did athletics. There wasn't a sense that he was going to be a world-renowned athlete. That only started revealing itself when he left school,' says Cameron.

However, Froome's popularity in a team environment and his quiet leadership skills did start to become evident during his school years. He was a boarder at Nash House and was selected as a house prefect. And he took it upon himself to start the school's first cycling club. 'He was really a motivating force in starting the cycling club, and remained a driving force within it. And as a house prefect, he was very respected and well liked by the other boys,' says Cameron.

It was in this boarding house that Froome first encountered and fell in love with the Tour de France. In his room, at the end of the corridor, he kept his bike and stationary rollers on which the bike would stand with its wheels raised off the floor to allow him to train indoors in poor weather. His former housemaster, Allan Laing, recalls how he would hear Froome spinning away on the training rollers at all hours. 'In the mornings, the afternoons, the evenings, you'd hear him. While other boys sat in the common room watching television, he was in his room pedalling his bicycle,' Laing told the *Guardian*.

The one time Froome did sit riveted to the television, though, was during the Tour de France. Laing allowed Froome to watch the Tour de France for the first time in 2002. It was a seminal moment. This was the first time that the boy who had had a burning desire for a bicycle saw the ultimate expression of this passion.

'It was in the boarding house at school where I first watched the Tour de France on TV and I just remember being blown away watching the guys racing up the mountains and thinking, "Wow, that would be amazing if I could get there one day",' he told the media during the 2013 Tour de France.

Laing, though, was at the time more concerned with Froome's education. 'Needs to take his academics as seriously as his cycling,' he wrote in one of Froome's reports.

Alan Lion-Cachet, the director of sport at St John's College, also recalls a happy, well-liked boy who stood out more for being a balanced, solid individual than a particularly talented sportsman. 'Chris was always very positive. He always had a big smile on his face and he participated in everything at the school. He could be a team person as well as an individual, and although quiet, he did have a big group of friends. Like all boys, he had a bit of mischief in him, but nothing too naughty.' Froome was not averse to using his knowledge of bicycles to offer bike-repair services to the woman who ran the senior boarding house for girls. These were the only girls at St John's, and Froome used the opportunity to meet some of them.

As well as his love for cycling, Lion-Cachet recalls Froome's impressive athletic ability. 'He played in the backline in rugby, but he was quite a small boy so rugby wasn't really his game. But he was very good at cross-country. I watched him win the inter-house cross-country title at the school.'

Froome took his idea of starting a cycling club at St John's to Lion-Cachet:

When he was in grade 9, he came to me with this idea for a cycling club. He was really driven and knew what he wanted to do with it. We didn't offer cycling as a school sport because we generally focus on sports that offer us fixtures against other schools. But we had a cultural period every Tuesday and Thursday for the last hour of school, so we allowed Chris to start the cycling club during that time. He started it with his friend Matthew Beckett, who was also a keen cyclist.

Froome and Beckett, the son of South African journalist and author David Beckett, spent a lot of time cycling together, and even at this point there was a growing indication of where the dedication lay with the two of them. Beckett gave up cycling shortly after school. 'I think he realised he didn't have the same potential as Chris,' says Lion-Cachet.

It's a sentiment confirmed by Beckett. 'It was obvious straight away that he was better than any of us would ever be,' he told the *Guardian*. 'Watching all of this happen for him kind of makes me wish I'd kept going, but I know I would never have got to his level. Not even close.'

Beckett experienced this first-hand during a training camp with Froome in 2004 in Mpumalanga. He was perhaps the first to witness the early development of Froome's incredible endurance and raw strength on a bicycle:

We were staying at the top of this mountain pass, but over the course of the first day I got a stomach bug and I was so weak, stopping to run into the bushes every five minutes. We were stuck in the middle of nowhere, it was starting to get dark and we didn't have any cellphone reception or anything. He told me not to worry, and to hold on to the back of his shirt, and then he pulled both of us up this mountain so much faster than I ever would have gone myself.

The two of them shared a love for similar sports at school and are photographed standing next to each other in one of the school's athletics team photographs. But in several photos, Froome appears with his head slightly bowed and often looking off to the side with an almost whimsical smile on his face, rather than adopting the cocksure pose of many young schoolboys revelling in their athletic prowess.

Perhaps it had something to do with being a child who, although he had loving parents, was largely left to his own devices. While Froome was at St John's, his father did not take an active part in his school life. 'Chris never had pushy parents,' says Lion-Cachet. 'His dad would come to some of the big events at the school, but nothing more than this. He was never hovering around Chris all the time. So Chris just got on and did it himself. He knew how to stand on his own two feet.'

Froome was happy to fill any spare gaps in his school schedule with his passion, cycling, and Beckett recalls how it began to dominate his friend's life. 'He won most of the running races he took part in. But with all the cycling we did, he and I would get into trouble for not getting involved in many of the other school sports – we barely had time for anything else beyond cycling and study. He played competitive paintball for a while, though. He had a few guns and used to enjoy shooting his mates – and also from time to time his brother, though I'll get into trouble for saying so.'

The two school friends have remained close. Beckett travelled to Paris for the finish of the 2013 Tour de France and was among the first to congratulate his old friend.

During his school days, Froome spent the greatest part of

his time, often alone, on the roads in the area, honing his cycling skills. He would take himself as far as Hartbeespoort Dam and Hekpoort, and the hills of Bronkhorstspruit and Bapsfontein.

Froome also immersed himself actively in the South African racing scene. 'The great thing about South African cycling is that there is an event every week. You didn't have to be a pro ... you could just stick a number on and ride. It was an essential part of my development as a cyclist, even though the racing didn't suit me. But training at altitude was a huge factor, and helped me a lot when I eventually went over to Europe,' he told *Bicycling* magazine editor, Mike Finch.

Lion-Cachet recalls how Froome would rise early in the morning before school to cycle. 'He'd cycle down the M1 highway towards Midrand, much to the frustration of the Metro Police. A master would come fetch him if his bike broke down. He also spent a lot of time cycling in the local gym.'

At the gym, some of Froome's friends decided to pull a prank on him, not knowing how close to the truth they were to come. 'Chris was riding a spinning bike in the gym, and some of the boys decided to go there and surprise him,' recalls Lion-Cachet. One of the boys was Scott Spedding, a South African rugby player who has spent most of his rugby career in France. 'They snuck up behind Chris and then jumped in front of his spinning bike. They were squirting these water bottles in his face and cheering and shouting, "C'mon, Chris. You're winning the Tour de France. Keep going, buddy."'

Froome's passion for cycling was certainly picked up by

all of those around him, but there was still never an indication at this stage that it was anything more than a schoolboy obsession. Not even to a man with a trained eye for such things.

'I've been involved at all levels of sport,' says Lion-Cachet, who played provincial-level hockey, achieved senior provincial colours for athletics and national colours for sailing. 'You see potential in a boy, but you never know where they're going to end up. A lot of it's about commitment. The desire must be there, and the sacrifice. Chris showed a lot of endurance ability, and from a cycling perspective he obviously had a passion for his sport. But at the start, when you saw Chris you wouldn't say he was going to win the Tour de France one day.'

During the 2013 Tour de France, St John's celebrated every victory Froome achieved on his way to overall glory. 'The television in our sport director's office was on all the time, and we had a few staff members who had to have urgent meetings there,' says headmaster Cameron. 'The whole school followed his progress with great excitement. Hopefully, we had an impact on the character he showed during that race. But, to be honest, I'm a little embarrassed to claim too much of his achievement because I think it rests largely with him.'

On the day before the final stage of the 2013 Tour de France, the school celebrated Froome's inevitable victory with what they called Froome Friday. The boys and staff wore yellow jerseys to school, and they followed the age-old tradition of ringing the victory bell in recognition of a major triumph from one of their old boys.

And the victory of the St John's alumnus has travelled around the world. 'We recently enrolled a boy from the United States. His mom said she'd seen our school on television there because of what Chris Froome achieved,' says Cameron.

The streets of Houghton have their own stories to tell of the young boy who cycled his heart out there. One of Froome's favourite climbs was the historic Munro Drive, a major landmark in Upper Houghton that offers incredible views of Johannesburg. And it seems strangely apt that Froome should spend his school years cycling up this stretch of road. It was built by Italian prisoners of war, who were captured by the South African forces during the Allied campaign in North Africa in World War II and sent to South Africa. (More than 60 000 Italians were held in South Africa.) Froome cycled a road built by many of these men from the country that has produced such champion cyclists as Gino Bartali, twice winner of the Tour de France – but, more significantly, a man who secretly sheltered Jews when the Nazis occupied Italy in World War II and who smuggled counterfeit identity documents hidden in his bicycle, which were used to conceal the true identity of many Jewish families, who were able to avoid persecution as a result.

And the country of Fausto Coppi, Bartali's greatest rival and the first man to win the Tour de France and the Giro d'Italia double in 1949 and 1952 – and an admitted user of a drug cocktail he called *la bomba*. Coppi was himself a prisoner of war in North Africa, at one stage working as a barber for British officers, who had no inkling of the legendary status he held in his home country.

Froome says he now recalls Munro Drive as nothing more than a speed bump compared with the mountains he cycled up during the Tour de France. But it was a road paved with its own piece of cycling history – one in which he too would soon take his own place.

Higher education

'Chris certainly didn't strike me
as anything special on the bike.'

Froome's career could have come to a tragic end during his first year at the University of Johannesburg. In 2005 he enrolled for a degree in economics. He seemed set to follow the career path of his two brothers, Jonathan and Jeremy, who are both chartered accountants. Froome has often joked that it was his fear of becoming the third chartered accountant in the family that made him pedal harder during training.

At university, cycling continued to dominate his thoughts. He was still not a very technically accomplished rider, but his understanding of the sport and the science behind it was growing.

'He was very meticulous in his preparation,' says Karel Mouton, the University of Johannesburg's cricket and cycling manager, and the man who remembers well the day it could have all ended for Froome on a tour to Cape Town.

With Froome's help, Mouton had assembled a team to

represent the university at the University Sports of South Africa's three-day tour in Cape Town. The team captain's mother had generously arranged for a minibus for the team to travel in, as well as accommodation in Cape Town. Says Mouton:

> We were just outside Beaufort West at around dusk, and Chris was with some of the other boys having fun in the back of the bus. His mom, Jane, had joined us as the team physiotherapist. Then, out of nowhere, a young kudu bull ran into the road. It hit the passenger side of our vehicle, and the car was a write-off.
>
> Fortunately nobody was hurt because there was nobody sitting in the passenger seat. But the car was destroyed. We had to look for accommodation for the night, and then had to arrange for a charter bus to come and fetch us in Beaufort West and take us to Cape Town.

It was a traumatic start to a tour in which Froome showed little of his potential on the bike. The event included an 80-kilometre road race and then an afternoon hill climb on day one, a 120-kilometre road race on day two, and then a time trial followed by a criterium on day three. For most of the competition, Froome was nowhere near being in contention. But then Mouton recalls how he suddenly came to the fore in the time trial. 'He was out of it, and then suddenly he did really well in the time trial and forced his way onto the podium. He finished third overall. But it was a low-key tour consisting mainly of students and only one or two professional riders. Chris certainly didn't strike me as anything special on the bike.'

But the tour did reveal other key ingredients in Froome's development as a cyclist – his attention to detail and willingness to make the kind of small, incremental changes that would later, at Team Sky, become the team's motto in their pursuit of excellence. Froome's discipline is what makes him such a perfect fit for Sky, who are meticulous in their planning and require Froome to follow their training instructions to the letter.

But on this tour, that same quality almost drove Mouton mad. The Cape Town tour ended the week before the Tour de France started. Mouton recalls how the young students on his team were all reading various magazines about the tour, and discussing every aspect of it:

Chris was very interested in how Lance Armstrong prepared for the tour in terms of his diet and so on. Unfortunately, we all know now that the magazine Chris was reading wouldn't be worth a cent – because Armstrong's diet wasn't the real story. But, at the time, Chris read anything he could about Armstrong's diet. He was incredibly meticulous like this. I got quite annoyed with him because we arrived in Cape Town and we were staying at this beautiful four-star hotel, which for these students was amazing. But Chris had me asking the chefs if they had green pasta and low GI food, for goodness' sake. Not even the chefs knew what he wanted. So here I was running around Cape Town trying to find green pasta for Chris. He never demanded anything. That wasn't his way. He was softly spoken, so it was more like an urgent request. And if I couldn't get it for him, he just said he'd go and find it himself. I had all the other students eating themselves full on this great food in the hotel, but Chris wouldn't touch it.

It was pure chance that Mouton crossed paths with Froome. You have to contact the cricket club at the University of Johannesburg to get hold of this man, who rode with and played a small role in the development of the future Tour de France winner. And that's because Mouton is a cricket manager first and recreational cyclist second. Beyond an ability to run around the streets of Cape Town searching for green pasta, Mouton is the first to tell you that he knows very little about professional cycling. 'Cycling was considered a minor sport at the university – and you know how it goes. They divide those smaller sports up among all of the staff, and I got the job.'

Mouton would arrange a few student rides now and again, and this is how he first met Froome. Today Mouton can look back and declare he is one of the few to have had the chance to cycle with a future Tour de France champion.

'Chris would arrive in his Hi-Q Academy team kit and join us for the rides. I remember there was one ride I did just with him. It was a rainy morning, and the other guys never turned up. But Chris was there, so off we went. We rode around Krugersdorp. We didn't really talk much because I was huffing and puffing just trying to keep up, and I think he was keeping a really slow pace for my benefit.'

When he looks back now, though he didn't recognise it at the time, Mouton feels that so much of what he didn't understand about Froome then now makes sense:

When we arrived back from that Cape Town tour, it was the last I ever saw of Chris. He spent about a year and a half with us at the university. He didn't fail economics – he just discontinued his studies. I think on that tour, the picture started to really form in his mind as to his becoming a professional cyclist. I tried to contact him a few times after that, just to find out how he was doing, but whenever I phoned he was out somewhere on his bicycle. And always alone. It all makes sense now. He knew what he needed to do. He knew he had no time for his studies and he'd made his choice. Somewhere on that tour, the seed was sown in him.

Teams and dreams

'Is he any good?'
'Sure he is. He's just having a bad day.'

Gareth Edwards was driving the team car for the Hi-Q Academy during the mountain stage of the Tour of Tzaneen. With him was Jane Froome, who had made the trip from Kenya to watch her son compete for Hi-Q. It was the first time she had seen him take part in a major stage race. Jane had decided to make a holiday of it. But on this day, she was worried. Chris didn't seem to be performing particularly well.

Edwards remembers the day. 'On about stage 4,' he says, 'Chris wasn't having a good day, and up one of the big climbs he was being shelled [a rider who is having difficulty keeping up with the pace of the peloton].'

Jane was sitting in the back seat. At one point, she leant forward and asked Edwards, 'Is he any good?' Edwards was stumped for an answer. 'Sure he is,' he told Jane. 'He's just having a bad day.'

But Edwards had his doubts. 'Chris wasn't anything great. He was built like a cyclist, but he wasn't exceptional. Look, by South African standards, he was fine. He would finish with the front boys, but he'd never try to do anything to get anybody's attention.'

Now a respected television news anchor in South Africa, Edwards had worked with Froome when he rode for his first two amateur teams in South Africa – Super C and then the Hi-Q Academy. To him, Froome was a slightly awkward character – the guy with fluffy hair whose clothes didn't fit properly – the one who had that streak of mischief about him, but who never let it stray to the point of ever being rude or disrespectful. 'He was always the first one to hold down the newbies in the team and shave their heads, and he would steal things from other guys' bags and hide them. He had a great sense of humour.'

But what Jane was asking of him was a deeper assessment of her son's potential. Was Chris's talent able to match his passion? Edwards didn't have the answer, and neither did Froome, he believed. 'I think for a very long time, even Chris didn't know how good he was, or could become.'

It's a familiar theme among those who knew Froome in his early days in South Africa. 'To be honest, he was very average,' says Andrew McLean, one of South Africa's leading cyclists, who was also involved with the Hi-Q Academy and went on to open the popular Cycle Lab store in Johannesburg:

Chris came to Hi-Q towards the end of his school career. He didn't stand out in any way in terms of his cycling potential. His bike-handling skills weren't great. His only characteristic was he was hard-working and well mannered. He was the guy you wanted your daughter to come home with, but his cycling ability was nothing to get excited about.

If you asked me then, I would've said he didn't have what it takes to make it, and I would've been so wrong. If you'd asked me about Robert Hunter, I would've said there's a guy who can make it. Robert is angry and a fighter. He's got it. But, with Chris, I would've bet my house on him not making it in pro cycling. I've never seen a success story like this in my life. I think it gives such hope to other young cyclists out there, because here's a guy who early in his career couldn't win a race even if you paid off half the peloton.

It seems a harsh assessment of Froome, who, in the opinion of McLean and a few others, was no more than a solid *domestique* (a support rider for the leader in a team). And that's the strategy Konica Minolta had in mind when they picked him up and he signed for them – his first professional cycling team.

'You had the feeling Chris was never going to win anything big. It was his ability as a worker that stood out. He was always an unbelievably hard worker,' says McLean. Yet for those around him with an eye for such things, even this aspect of Froome's psyche was admired more as a pleasing character trait of a nice young man, rather than a sign it would lead to a successful career as a professional cyclist.

'At Cycle Lab we had an indoor training facility. Chris

would often come there to train. I'd walk past him and he would be on the bike tapping out his kilometres and doing hours and hours of training, and I thought, "Well, that's nice." But I never imagined anything more would come of it.'

McLean draws attention to another element he felt was lacking in Froome for him to rise to the pinnacle of world cycling. In short, McLean thought he was just too nice to be a winner – he didn't have that ruthless edge about him:

> Chris doesn't have the personality of a winner. For a start, he's as honest as the day is long. In cycling, to be a winner you have to be ruthless and stand on a few people. Chris is not like that at all. Other riders will quickly tell journalists to fuck off if they ask the wrong or difficult questions, but Chris would never do that. What you saw during the 2013 Tour de France, with him enduring all those tough questions about doping over and over again and remaining calm about it, that's Chris. That's his natural personality. I mean, when Bradley Wiggins was asked about doping early in the 2012 Tour de France, he flipped. But Chris endured it for three weeks. He doesn't have the obvious qualities of a winner.

But Froome's lack of overt ruthlessness is not to say he doesn't have it inside. Froome hides very well an ambitious streak and a steely determination. He is the baby-faced assassin of his sport – the one the peloton never saw coming. Today, Froome says all of the right things off the bike, and then does all of the right things on it as well.

And his perceived lack of a win-at-all-costs mentality has convinced those closest to him that the doping allegations that dogged him during the 2013 Tour de France are unfounded. Says Edwards:

> Not Chris Froome. He wouldn't dare. He's too honest and doesn't have it in him to lie. He doesn't have the personality traits of a doper. Chris is not a desperate kind of character. The guys that get on the drugs are the desperate guys. Chris is also young enough to have avoided the Lance Armstrong and Tyler Hamilton sagas. I think Chris has shown that the biological passport actually works. He's never had any suspicious test results, and I believe this new generation of cycling is absolutely clean. I'm sure Chris was approached to dope, just as every cyclist has been approached. South African cyclist Malcolm Lange once told me he was approached and said no, and I believe Chris would've done the same if he'd been asked.

This is the mantle that Chris Froome carries: the nice guy who is able to win the world's toughest bike race while remaining polite and clean. He is everything Lance Armstrong was not.

Nevertheless, he is as calculating as anyone about what he needs to do to be the best. For example, he has always been obsessed with the science behind cycling – the numbers and stats that make professional cycling arguably the most scientifically analysed of all sports. Froome was one of the first South African cycling pros to start training according to power output, using technology such as power meters rather than heart-rate measurements. A power meter is a device that measures the rider's power output. It is fitted to the crankset of the bike, and a display unit on the handlebars gives the rider information such as an instant burst of power, and maximum and average power. The technology gives the rider a more objective and accurate picture of his power output than a heart-rate monitor is able to. The feedback is also more instantaneous and less affected by environmental conditions such as weather, fluctuating heart rate, and so on. It's a pure form of analysis and allows a cyclist's training to be more finely tracked and monitored. Froome was convinced power monitoring was the way to train, rather than the traditional heart-rate model.

The cleaning up of cycling in terms of drugs has been used as an explanation for how Froome might have seemed average when he was younger but then went on to become a serious contender in cycling's grand tours. 'When Chris was riding in Europe on bread and water [known as *paniagua* among European cyclists], every other pro was taking dope,' explains McLean. 'Once everybody had cleaned up and came back three steps, Chris looked really good. He went from the middle of the peloton to the front.'

Froome has spent most of his later career riding in the so-called clean era of the Tour de France.

* * *

Another man who believes Froome is a 100 per cent clean cyclist is Gavin Cocks:

He was so anti-doping ever since he arrived in Europe in 2008. When we used to go out for dinner together, he'd take his own cup of lentils with him, which he'd grown himself. I think it must have been very difficult for him to convey the anti-doping message during the 2013 tour. But I know Chris would definitely never get involved in doping. I think the best thing was that he cracked the second time going up Alpe d'Huez. It showed he was human and, yes, he had a breakdown there. But I believe in the long run, Chris is going to put Lance Armstrong to shame with his ability to win five, six, seven or more Tours de France clean. He's only 28 years old now, so he's got the time.

Cocks is passionate in his support of Froome. Theirs has been, and still is, a very close relationship. Cocks owned the Hi-Q tyre franchise in Nelspruit. His son, Edwin, was a passionate cyclist, and Gavin shared his son's interest. Together with Robbie Nilsen, an attorney in Johannesburg, whose son also rode, he formed the Hi-Q Academy in 2002, with Cocks as the main sponsor and Nilsen as the coach. Nilsen, who still does some legal work for Froome, had to turn down a request to be interviewed for this book. But Cocks spoke openly, warmly and emotionally about the cyclist whom he clearly views as if he were his own son. 'The team was really just a couple of parents funding it ourselves for our boys,' says Cocks. They began with under-16 cyclists, and then in 2004 began to include junior riders. That year they took their team to compete in the Tour of Lesotho, which is where they first met Froome.

Froome had come to the mountainous kingdom of Lesotho to compete with the Super C team. On one of the mountain stages, he rode next to some of the Hi-Q riders, and afterwards approached Cocks and Nilsen with the idea of introducing an under-23 team at Hi-Q.

'We explained to Chris that our focus wasn't on creating cyclists at all costs. Our kids still had to continue with their schooling and play other sports as well. It wasn't just about the cycling. We had a long-term plan. But Chris liked that plan. He said he would find the riders for an under-23 team, so we gave it a try,' says Cocks.

Froome, Cocks and Nilsen would go on to develop a very close bond, which they still have to this day. Froome became a part of their families, particularly Cocks's:

> When he came to our home, you could see he really wanted to be there. My wife, Wanda, was always so impressed with how helpful he was. He would always help wash up after a meal, and he'd even help prepare the food. I always got the sense that he would give away what he had just to make someone else happy. He was just such a good kid. I always admired the way he was going to university and how he would put his training schedules together to balance his study time. He was so dedicated.

Cocks remembers Froome's desire to understand what he was doing with his training rather than just blindly following the pack. And he was patient about how he wanted to get there. 'Chris was the kind of person who wanted to understand why he was improving, or why he wasn't,' says Cocks.

When Froome's mother passed away in 2008, Cocks saw another side of the young man. Cocks had also had a bereavement – he lost his son – and the two grew even closer. 'Chris is a very deep thinker and a spiritual person. After 2008, when he was starting to do well in Europe, he would always say he knew he had two other people there with him – his mom and my son.'

Cocks is one of the few with whom Froome shared his deepest feelings about his mother's death, perhaps sensing a kinship with a man who had experienced and understood such a loss. Froome does not speak much about his parents publicly, and even less about his mother, with whom he spent the greater part of his childhood. He dedicated his Tour de France victory to his mother, but beyond this hasn't spoken much of how her death affected him, or perhaps drove him to achieve. It bears a striking resemblance to the career of South African golf legend, Gary Player, who, like Froome, also lost his mother to cancer at an early age. The death forged an independence in the golfer, but it also left a hole he has spent most of his life trying to fill. His drive to become a world champion included a desire to keep proving to his mother that he had done well in her absence. He played for a mother who was never there to see his greatest moments, and the memory of her death still haunts him. Even late into his career, he would often wake up in the middle of the night crying at her loss. There is a similar sense that what drives Froome up the mountains is the desire to answer the question Jane had asked Gareth Edwards in that Tzaneen team event: 'Is he any good?'

When Froome was invited to join the Konica Minolta team in 2007, he remained in touch with Cocks and would often stay with him during training camps. 'Chris would tell us stories about the new team and how his teammates thought he was mad because of how much he was training and his dedication to cycling. They thought he'd burn out.'

And Cocks remembers how Froome remained drawn to the mountains. 'Sometimes he and a friend would come and visit us. They'd get up at about eight in the morning and ride for the whole day. They'd come home and Chris would tell us how they found this awesome mountain and did their own time trials up and down it. Another time, they arrived back from their ride in a delivery truck. They had been training so hard that they absolutely cracked [ran out of energy] and had to catch a lift back.'

When Froome had signed on with Sky, among the first people he contacted were Cocks and Nilsen.

He said to me, 'Gavin, my aim is to be a GC [general classi-fication] contender in the Tour de France within five years.' At the time, I thought that was a massive goal. Yet two years after joining the team, he was a GC contender, and then a year later he was a Tour de France winner.

I don't know what it takes to become so good in cycling, and even at Hi-Q I wasn't so sure. But we did believe that if anybody was going to achieve our dream of a Tour de France rider, then it was Chris.

Froome has remained loyal to those who helped him. In his office, Cocks has a framed email Froome sent him in March 2010 titled 'Living the dream'. Froome had sent it when he first started to taste success in Europe. He had written about how he could still not believe he was competing against some of the big names in cycling – and sometimes even beating them.

If you are to go by Froome's own words in this email, his growing success in the sport came as a surprise even to him. 'If you'd told me a few years ago I would be dropping great names like these on climbs I'd have told you to turn over,' he wrote.

Then Cocks breaks into tears as he recalls the last part of the email. 'Chris said he was living the dream, but that none of it would've been possible if it hadn't been for the support we had given him. He went on to say how thankful he was for that support and that he would never forget us.'

Cocks sounds like a proud father as he singles out moments that reveal more about the character of Froome than his cycling ability:

When Chris was doing so well in the 2013 Tour de France, I phoned Robbie and said, 'C'mon, let's go over there and surprise him.' Robbie was keen, but then he couldn't make it. So I went on my own for the final day. I stood in the Champs Élysées from 8 a.m. and watched the whole finish. I was impressed by the fact that when he was on the podium he turned to acknowledge the general crowd as well, not just the VIPs. By about 11.15 that night, I still hadn't managed to see Chris, and thought I wasn't going to get the chance. So I made my way back to the train.

It was then that Cocks heard a roar from the crowd as Froome emerged from the media tent, having completed his interviews. Cocks spotted Matthew Beckett with Froome.

'I called out to Matt, who recognised me. And Matt tapped Chris on the shoulder and pointed me out to him. Chris broke away from the escort and came to greet me. He thanked me for supporting him all those years. The winner of the Tour de France – that's a sign of the type of guy he is.'

Froome's mentor, David Kinjah, witnessed a similar development of this side of the sportsman's personality. In 2004, when Kinjah had entered the newly launched Cape Epic mountain-bike race in South Africa, Froome phoned him to say he had made good contacts in South Africa and would be able to get Kinjah's air ticket sponsored. He also spoke to Kinjah about an idea he had for a charity bike ride from Kenya to South Africa to help fund the work of the Safari Simbaz club. And he was trying to put together a team of young black South African cyclists. Kinjah recalls:

He said they were a little lazier than the Kenyans. He asked me to come to South Africa to speak to them and show them how to be something. He said, 'Kinjah, you're the perfect example for these kids. You'll show them how to work hard.' He wanted me to come and stay with him in South Africa. But I told him I couldn't leave Kenya because what would happen to Kenyan cycling? He even tried to get me a place on the Konica Minolta team he was riding for at that stage. I thanked him, but I told him I'm sure they weren't interested in me because I was too old. I said to him, 'Chris, don't worry about me. You go for it.' But that showed me the kind of person he was becoming. He was never selfish.

But, as far as his cycling potential was concerned, Froome had still not shown even his closest friends a glimpse of the force he would become. To a large extent, this had nothing to do with his talent, and everything to do with where he was living.

The South African road-racing scene is very small. The race distances are typically around 100 kilometres and generally flat, so they suit the sprinters more than the climbers. If you can't sprint, you can't win. And Froome couldn't sprint. He has what in cycling terms is referred to as an incredible engine, and he possesses a power-to-weight ratio that makes him extremely strong on the bike. This is why he can perform so well in the mountains.

It is significant that the few triumphs Froome enjoyed during his time in South Africa included the 2006 Jock race around the mountainous region of Nelspruit, and victory on the fairly mountainous route of the Tour of Mauritius. Those races suited Froome's style, and were the only time he revealed anything of his potential. But, for the most part, the racing style in South Africa just didn't suit Froome.

During his time in South Africa, Froome started to model himself on South African star cyclist Robbie Hunter, who had achieved the holy grail of a successful career in Europe. But many remained sceptical of Froome's ability to follow a man such as Hunter. The gritty South African was for many years Africa's greatest hope in European cycling, and it was tough even for him to break through. According to Kinjah,

Chris was trying to imitate Hunter. Hunter was a big name and was trying to get to the tour as well, but it was hard even for him. I had raced with Robert in the Commonwealth Games and was with the breakaway in 1998 in Kuala Lumpur. He was the young star. We rode so hard, and he joined me in the breakaway and said, 'C'mon, we must ride hard for Africa.' But I just couldn't go any more, and eventually he couldn't either. We both didn't finish the race. Then along comes Chris Froome, a Kenyan. Why would we ever think of him and the Tour de France?

When asked whether he had ever seen anything that suggested to him that Froome might just be able to make it as a professional, Kinjah points to the 2006 Commonwealth Games in Australia. Both he and Froome, racing under the Kenyan flag, were in the breakaway. At one point during the race, when the breakaway was brought back, Froome attacked and was in front for a while. But Australia's Mathew Hayman took the gold in 4:05:09. Froome finished 25th, just over five minutes behind Hayman, and Kinjah finished 27th.

But, increasingly, there was a focus developing in Froome as he reached the end of his time with the Hi-Q Academy and began thinking seriously about a professional career. The amount of time he spent on his sport and the questioning from his parents as to where it was all headed were forcing him towards a crossroads. Ironically, it may have been a serious injury that eventually helped him make the decision to pursue his dream rather than take up a regular job.

Froome crashed during a training ride and broke his collarbone. He was sidelined for six weeks, but it didn't stop him training. He took his bike to the indoor facility at Cycle Lab, put it on a stationary trainer and continued to follow his full training programme. The training schedule that needs to be put in by top cyclists makes it one of the most mentally challenging sports and demands a high level of dedication. To cycle six or seven hours a day on the road is hard enough; to do so on a stationary trainer – with not even the sights and sounds of the outdoors as a distraction – is excruciatingly boring. Yet Froome was happy to commit to it, and he rode thousands of kilometres on the trainer with his arm in a sling – literally going nowhere, yet travelling deep into the realisation that he had an endurance capacity to carry him to the furthest physical limits required by his sport. That was a major mental switch for Froome. It was the key moment that he began to realise he could endure the suffering – a quality he would surely need for the Tour de France, a mental quality that American rider Tyler Hamilton, legendary for his ability to endure pain before he became embroiled in doping with Lance Armstrong, described as requiring 'an unimaginable level of strength, toughness and suffering'. Hamilton set the benchmark for suffering on a bicycle. He fractured his shoulder during a crash in the 2002 Giro d'Italia, yet rode on, grinding 11 of his teeth down to the roots as he pushed through the pain. And he finished second. Then, in the 2003 Tour de France, Hamilton fractured his collarbone. He rode on, winning a stage and finishing fourth overall.

With his own arm in a sling, Froome was learning how to suffer with the best of them.

Goodbye, Kenya

'We thought, "That guy's got something, for sure."'

Charles Mose, the secretary general of the Kenya Cycling Federation (KCF), is doing his best to sound positive about all of this. Despite the fact that so many Kenyans hold him and the KCF responsible for letting Chris Froome slip through their fingers and into the waiting arms of Britain. 'We encouraged Chris to join a good team, where he would have much better equipment than we could give him,' Mose says.

But many Kenyans feel it was more a case of Froome's own hand being forced in the matter. As his appetite for cycling grew and he began to seek greater goals for himself, he started experiencing the frustration of being a leading cyclist for his home country of Kenya, where what little money there is for sports development is swallowed up by football and athletics. Froome's resourcefulness meant he was already hustling his way through international cycling, and with the minimum of support from the KCF.

Determined to compete in the 2006 under-23 World Time Trial Championships in Salzburg, but hampered by bureaucracy within the KCF, Froome hacked into the KCF's email account and logged an entry for himself. He would travel to Austria as the sole member of the Kenyan team. He would be the rider, manager and bike mechanic.

Froome arrived in Salzburg alone. Carrying his bike and his bags, he got lost trying to find his way to the team managers' meeting. When he did get there, drenched from rain, his bedraggled appearance aroused suspicion in the other managers, who duly informed him that the meeting was not open to riders. Froome informed them that he was the one-man Kenyan cycling army, and took his place in the room.

His debut in European road racing was equally inauspicious – about 150 metres into the time trial, he crashed into a race official. Froome went on to finish 36th in the race. That year he also competed in the Commonwealth Games for Kenya. While many say they never spotted Froome's true potential, his experience in the 2006 Commonwealth Games was significant, in that it provided Froome's future Tour de France Sky team manager and performance director of British Cycling, David Brailsford, with his first glimpse of the rider from Africa. In particular, his performance during the elite men's time trial caught Brailsford's attention. Brailsford told *VeloNews*:

> He didn't have the best equipment. I watched his time trial; this was a guy from nowhere, he did this phenomenal performance. I was like, 'Bloody hell, who is this guy?' That was the first time I ever saw him ... The performance he did, on the equipment he was on, that takes some doing. We thought, 'That guy's got something, for sure.' We always thought he was a bit of a diamond in the rough, who had a huge potential ... From [the Commonwealth Games] we opened lines of communication with him. It went from there.

The organisational frustrations he was experiencing and the possibility of acquiring British citizenship through his parents meant it was only natural that Froome began to consider this option. And his mentor, Kinjah, fully supported his decision. 'There was already a lot of frustration and a lot of politics in the federation [the KCF],' Kinjah explained in an interview with Kenyan radio station CapitalFM.

So in 2007, Froome raced for the last time under the Kenyan flag in the All-Africa Games in Algeria. He claimed bronze in the road race, with South Africa's Daryl Impey taking gold. That year, he decided to turn professional and received his first break when he joined the Konica Minolta team in South Africa. Kinjah explains:

> It was frustrating for him. He decided he didn't want to participate in the politics, he wanted to go ahead and realise his dreams and goals. His mother passed away and the little bit of hope left for him disappeared ... For Chris, it was most important that what he had built with a lot of challenges did not disappear and the British were already knocking on the door. They had already seen the problems, frustrations and mismanagement in Kenya and they showed Chris his future was not here. It was up to Chris to make up his mind and they asked him, 'Do you want to stay a Kenyan and lose it all or do you want to go ahead and get support?' He chose option B, and to me, he made a good choice: he had nothing to lose.

Mose tries his best not to sound bitter when it comes to the subject of Froome's change of citizenship:

In Kenya, our riders are using bikes that weigh 8 to 10 kilograms and that cost maybe $2 000. Still to this day, we are of the opinion that if there is a good opportunity, our athletes should go for it. South Africa did so much for Chris in helping him have access to better equipment. The Kenya Cycling Federation does what it can. We are supported by personal contributions from the members of the executive, and we get a lot of help from other countries and federations, and so on. Believe me, if we had everything South Africa offered Chris, then he would never have had to leave Kenya. Then he took British citizenship and that was also good for him.

In an interview with *Cycling Weekly* in 2008, Froome explained his own reasons behind his decision. 'Almost all my family have left Kenya. I barely have any connections with the place, and I left there for South Africa when I was a young teenager ... Secondly, I am British by blood; that's where my grandparents come from and still live ... One of my brothers is living in London, too. Thirdly, the infrastructure and support which British Cycling can give me is much, much better than anything I could get from Kenya. It all added up, basically.'

In another interview, with *Cyclingnews*, after riding in his first Tour de France in 2008, Froome said: 'I'm not known in Kenya and I don't think anybody there will really hear about me riding the tour, except from my brother, who has returned and is living in Nairobi, where I rode my first race. There aren't more than three or four races a year in Kenya. Bicycles are too expensive for the people. That's why they run, and they run so well.'

But the final decision was made after the death of Froome's mother in 2008 from bone-marrow cancer. With his last family link to Kenya now gone, Froome decided to take up British citizenship through his parents.

Jane was buried in Kenya, becoming a part of the hills he rode, the blue sky he lay and fished under, the wild animals he and David Kinjah cycled past, the country where a young boy first took a little BMX bike and cycled his way to the podium of the Tour de France.

Europe: Pizza and the plan

Chris Froome @chrisfroome   10 May 2013
Moving on up ...

(Tweeted as Froome was preparing for the 2012 Tour de France.)

The grand plan to take Chris Froome from a neo-pro in Europe to Tour de France champion was mapped out in a small restaurant in Chiari, a town near Brescia in north-west Italy. Over a pizza. 'It was a margherita,' remembers Alex Carera.

Carera was the agent for South African cyclist Robert Hunter. In his thick Italian accent, Carera recalls how, in early 2008, he sat with Hunter and the young rider whom Hunter had brought over from South Africa as part of Team Barloworld.

Hunter was already feted in Europe as the first South African to have competed in the Tour de France. That was in 2001. He was now the team leader of Barloworld, and in 2007 became the first South African to win a stage in the Tour de France, when he took stage 11 – Marseilles to

Montpellier. It was a significant moment for Hunter as the leader of a ramshackle team that had gained entry to the tour at the last minute as a wild card, but which built up tremendous respect for their performances during that tour.

Hunter also finished third in stage 12 and fourth in stage 20, but went on to finish only 118th overall behind champion Alberto Contador. Yet there was something prophetic about his words to the media following his stage-11 victory. Asked during the press conference about the state of cycling in South Africa, Hunter replied, 'The problem is there is not enough behind the sport in South Africa to bring it up to a professional level like it is in Europe. There are so many people who get to a good amateur level but the transition to becoming professional in Europe isn't there. Something like this I'm hoping will boost the sport in South Africa to get more young riders up to a professional level in Europe. We have so many young, talented riders that can perform at this level.'

One such rider was Froome, whom Hunter believed in. He wanted Europe to start believing in him as well.

Hunter and the hunted

'The first time I saw Chris ride was one of the races in South Africa, and he was a mess on a bike.'

When I speak to Robbie Hunter, he has just announced his retirement from professional cycling. Over the phone and during a wet and miserable Tour of Britain, the hard man of South African cycling says simply, 'I guess it's time.'

Hunter has been forced to call time on a 16-year career that saw him become the first South African to ride in the Tour de France and the first South African to win stages in all three of the grand tours – stage victories in the 2007 Tour de France, the 1999 and 2001 Vuelta a España, and the 2012 Giro d'Italia. Hunter also achieved a host of other accomplishments that have made him the face of African cycling for many years.

But the most successful South African road cyclist in history, who has ridden for eight teams since 1999, now has no team to call home. He was expecting an extension of his two-year contract with Team Garmin-Sharp before they changed their minds. 'I know I got the legs but I guess teams don't think so,' he tweeted.

As we speak, Hunter reveals the greatest disappointment of his career: not being able to ride in what would have been his tenth Tour de France, in 2014. The world's greatest cycle race has dished up its fair share of broken bones and heartache for Hunter. In common with all who have ridden it, the tour is the golden thread running through his career in Europe. And it remains responsible for the greatest disappointment of his career:

The hardest moment for me was stopping on my very first Tour de France. I had a whole bunch of friends come out and I messed up. I was 22 years old. You get ahead of yourself and you've got no idea what you're getting into. You're racing beyond your means every single day. I had nobody to guide me during the stages, telling me to take it easy here or go hard here. I raced every day like it was my last. I'm disappointed that I never finished my first Tour de France.

It feels so very wrong to be speaking to him about another African cyclist, to ask him to stop reflecting on his own greatest disappointment and focus instead on the man who achieved for African cycling what Robert Hunter worked and fought so hard for, and sacrificed so much for – victory in the Tour de France.

But Hunter is a pragmatic sportsman. In addition to achieving his own triumphs, he has spent the greater part of his professional career working for others in the pelotons of Europe. He knows that he has a job to do, and when your job is done, you have to move on. He did just such a job for Chris Froome, kicking down doors to open up the world of European cycling for the young African cyclist. And yet, if you were to think Hunter shares a special bond with Froome, you would be wrong.

We were never the best of friends. For a start, Chris is younger than me. I just put my hand out there to try and help the guy and felt he deserved the chance. There are not many guys I've ever put my hand in the fire for. But it's not like we've become great friends. I've never invited him around to my house for a whisky or anything. When we see each other, it's friendly, and when he moved to Monaco I helped him make a few decisions there. I think it's great what he's done. In my case, it's always great to say I was the first to do this or that. But I was also always the first to say I couldn't wait until other Africans came to Europe and started doing things in cycling. But at the end of the day, Chris is where he is because of himself.

To take the last modest sentence at his word would be to ignore the role Hunter played in helping Froome advance his career to the next level in Europe. And Hunter was one of the few to look beyond Froome's lack of technical skills on a bicycle and tactical nous, and spot the one thing in Froome he recognised in himself – a willingness to suffer.

'The first time I saw Chris ride was one of the races in South Africa, and he was a mess on a bike. To be honest, he's still a bit of a mess on the bike. He's not the poster boy of technique. He's got a very different style to most people. He's always riding with his head down, so sometimes he makes the mistake of riding into guys. But he's got his own style and it obviously works for him. He's worked with what he's got.'

But it was Froome's determination to make it as a professional cyclist that stood out more for Hunter. 'Mentally, I could see that he wanted to stay in Europe and would go to any extent to try and be a pro. He was okay with staying away from home for long periods of time. That made me realise he had something. Look, it's always up to the rider himself to decide how far he wants to go. But I knew Chris could be a proper professional.'

The biggest challenge for African cyclists in Europe is the lack of a support structure in terms of family and friends. There are still only a handful of African cyclists at the major races, and the language barrier makes it that much harder for them to settle down in Europe. For even the most talented of riders, it comes as quite a shock when suddenly their careers are no longer just about riding their bikes and coming home to a familiar environment and the full support of those around them: 'It's very hard in Europe. You've got nobody around you, and, even though it does get easier, it's still not home. I've seen a lot of South African riders come to Europe and then run away back home because they miss that support structure around them. I told Chris it wasn't going to be easy. I told him to start learning the languages in Italy and France because, when they see you are trying, that's how you start to make friends.'

So, a willingness for self-sacrifice, as opposed to obvious natural talent, is what made Hunter believe in Froome's potential. Yes, there were clearly signs that he could race well – Froome's results while with the UCI World Cycling Centre team, including victories in mountainous Italian races that are seen as the proving ground for young European professionals, had piqued Hunter's interest.

But, even when Froome was his teammate for Barloworld in the 2008 Tour de France, Hunter was still not overly impressed with his skills on a bike. 'Sure, he finished his first Tour de France, but I wasn't all that impressed. There wasn't that spark of presence like in the case of John-Lee Augustyn, who on his first tour showed flashes of brilliance on some of the climbs. Chris never did that. But it doesn't mean there wasn't anything there.'

It was purely thanks to Hunter that Froome made it into that Barloworld team. While the then team manager Claudio Corti is today quick to claim the credit for having recruited

Froome into the team, it is Hunter who in the end persuaded him by making countless phone calls to Corti:

> Claudio kept saying, 'Why should I sign a Kenyan rider?' I kept telling him that I knew what Chris was trying to do and he needed an opportunity. Here was a guy that was trying a lot harder than most other people to be a pro. I also told Claudio that Chris was a person who could finish on a podium in a grand tour. I said it because I believed it. Fortunately, Claudio listened to me. If he hadn't, I think Chris would've been lost in the system and ended up back in South Africa.

Staking his reputation on a young cyclist with no real credentials was risky. Predicting a podium finish in a grand tour for the same cyclist could easily have been described as insane, especially when you consider the physical sacrifice required to achieve such a feat.

★ ★ ★

Cycling's early history was not the same as the flashy, glamorous sport it has become today. Today recreational cycling is perceived as the new golf, with the thousands of men who get on their bikes for Saturday-morning rides referred to as MAMILs (middle-aged men in Lycra). But, in the early days, cyclists often rode not because they wanted to, but because they had to – to avoid starvation.

This aspect of cycling's history resonates with a cyclist such as Hunter. As recently as the 2010 Tour de France,

Hunter ended up throwing punches in the peloton as a result of what he called 'underhand tactics' by Danish rider Jakob Fuglsang. Hunter said Fuglsang hit him in the ribs when he had tried to pass him on the cobblestoned section of stage 3. 'He's got no right to put his hands on me,' Hunter told the media at the time. And he said the same to Fuglsang on the bike – in rather more abrupt terms, of course.

'Cycling was always a hard man's sport,' explains Hunter. 'It wasn't a rich man's sport like it is today. Those early cyclists would race around the church in Belgium to put food on the table. It wasn't like riding horses in the paddocks in the United Kingdom. So a lot of the guys that came to become good bikers were hard men.'

The French had a word for these Belgian farm boys who were as hard as nails. They called them *flahute* – tough guys from the Flemish north of the country. After World War II, scores of Belgian men had two options – they could either suffer in the fields or on a bicycle. Many chose the latter. A *flahute* in professional cycling is not necessarily the best rider. He's just the toughest. He's the one who rides the cobblestoned streets of Europe as if they were a smooth five-lane highway. He's the one who, when it's lashing down with rain and the wind is throwing buckets of water in your face, dons his cap and rides like it's a perfect summer's day. These are the men who in the history of the sport saw it as a sign of weakness to change to an easier gear during a climb. They would rather keep pounding away in the same gear. And when half the peloton bails or fails to finish a race, they are the minority who never quit, no matter what. There are hard men in cycling, and then there are *flahute.*

This physical element remains today in terms of the sheer endurance required to complete a Tour de France. As Hunter explains, the actual mileage of the race is not the challenge that the tour presents. Rather, it's the pace:

> You tell me to go and ride 3 000 kilometres in a month, and I'll do it. What makes the tour so much harder is that you're riding to the limits of the other riders. It's one thing pushing yourself to your own limits, and another pushing yourself to somebody else's limits. It's very difficult to explain to somebody who's never done it just how hard that is. That's what makes the tour the hardest thing in cycling by far. You're doing this every single day for three weeks. After week one, you're fatigued. By the end of week two, your body just wants to shut down because it's so tired. That's why I believe there are only four people in the world at any given time who can win a grand tour. It's a very select group of riders.

The authority and experience with which Hunter speaks is what made an agent like Alex Carera listen carefully when Hunter spoke to him of Froome. The story was certainly not unique. As an agent, Carera had had his fair share of people telling him they had just discovered the next best thing to ride a bicycle. But there was something he liked about Froome.

And it began with the pizza they were having: 'I meet with many young riders who are said to be great. I often go and have something to eat with them to see what they drink. The difference between a good rider and a great champion is seen not only on the bike, but off it as well. When a young rider has two beers while he is talking to me, I know we have a problem. Chris was just drinking water – so I knew he was serious.'

But it was just two words that convinced Carera that Froome was something special. Two words that had no usual place in professional cycling, and which many of the great and talented riders whom Carera had come into contact with did not utter – 'thank you'.

'Chris says thank you a lot. That's not normal, certainly not for the top riders. He wasn't normal like that. Chris is a very nice man. He is very polite. Whether it was another rider, a mechanic, the team staff, he always said thank you. He is very liked within the teams he works with.'

Having satisfied himself that Froome was someone he could work with, Carera explained to the young African how he believed they would arrive at the great goal – the Tour de France.

By mid-2008, Froome was there. And he was about to find out that getting to the Tour de France was one thing. Surviving it was something else altogether.

Le Tour

'This is the hardest thing I've ever done.
I don't know if I'll finish this race.'

At midnight on 27 July 2008, Kevin McCallum, the chief sports writer for the Independent Group of newspapers in

South Africa, stood on the Champs Élysées with a 23-year-old Chris Froome and his Barloworld teammate, John-Lee Augustyn.

The two riders had just finished their first Tour de France. It had been a steep learning curve for both, the most difficult part of which was dealing with the doping scandal that saw teammate Moisés Dueñas Nevado thrown out of the tour, along with four other riders, for doping. Froome was also dealing with the death of his mother five weeks earlier.

As McCallum recalls, for Froome and his team the goal for the 2008 Tour de France was simply to make it across the finishing line in one piece. Barloworld was a small team by tour standards, and it had just become smaller with the loss of the other teammates.

'There's this enduring image for me of these four guys left in the team and at one stage riding at the front of a 150-strong peloton. They impressed everybody with just how brave they were,' says McCallum.

Augustyn impressed on stage 16, when he made it to the top of the Col de la Bonette in the lead, but then crashed as he mistimed one of the hairpin bends on the descent of this mountain pass in the Alps. By the final stage, Froome and Augustyn were working hard to get their lead rider, Hunter, as near the front as they could. Hunter suffered a puncture and Froome handed him his own wheel. Hunter went on to finish tenth in the stage. Froome was obviously held up as he waited for a replacement wheel from the team car. 'I was standing there when Chris came over the finish line as well,' recalls McCallum. 'He was riding so hard, even though he was far behind. He was giving it his all, and the crowd showed their appreciation by giving him a huge round of applause.'

Froome later told McCallum that 'the stages towards the end were mostly survival for me at that point, but I had been quietly looking forward to the long final time trial. Finishing 16th there as a neo-pro did give me confidence for the future.'

McCallum also recognised the effect of that time-trial performance on Froome. 'When he finished 16th that day, you could see something was different about him.'

Most likely, it was the recognition that maybe, just maybe, he could do this. It was a massive revelation for Froome, because up until this point, he hadn't been convinced.

McCallum remembers how he had sat with Froome in the tiniest hotel room in Paris as the rider expressed his fear of not being up to the challenge of the Tour de France. Froome lay on the bed, wearing only his underpants and sporting red, sunburnt legs. He was sharing the room with Augustyn, and the accommodation dispelled any beliefs that being a cyclist in the Tour de France is a glamorous experience. Their two single beds were shunted up so close together that you couldn't even put your hand between them. He looked at McCallum and said, 'Kevin, this is the hardest thing I've ever done. I don't know if I'll finish this race.'

Then came that time trial, and suddenly Froome started to believe in himself. But it's not to say that his first Tour de France wasn't a harsh realisation that this was a race that would take everything from you and leave you drained both physically and mentally.

In the evening after the final stage, a boat cruise down

the Seine was laid on for the sponsors and riders. Froome and Augustyn arrived still in their team tracksuits, their bus having already left with all of their bags on board, but they were ready to let their hair down following a tumultuous first tour together. 'We were preparing for a big night on the town, and I remember laughing at the two of them sitting on that boat and smashing back glasses of wine. They were exhausted,' says McCallum.

After the cruise, the three of them went on a pub crawl around Paris. One of the nightclubs wouldn't allow them entry in their tracksuits, and Augustyn was willing to pay €300 to anybody who would sell them two pairs of pants. With no takers, they wandered around the streets of Paris soaking up the atmosphere and talking about their tour experience. Froome told McCallum repeatedly how tough the tour had been for him and how he hadn't been sure he would finish it.

A few years later, Froome explained to McCallum in more detail the fears he had harboured in the 2008 Tour de France. 'There were times I thought I may never get to the top of the sport and may have to reconsider my ambitions and settle for something a little more achievable.'

And based on his *palmarès* (cycling victories), Froome's fears weren't unrealistic. His was far from the traditional route to the Tour de France. His career path to the greatest bicycle race was more 'cosmopolitan', as the European media described it.

When Froome turned professional in 2007, having joined Team Konica Minolta, he only had a handful of minor victories in South Africa and Mauritius behind him. In 2007 he won a stage in the Tour of Japan and finished sixth overall. He also won the fifth stage of Italy's Giro delle Regioni stage race. In 2008 he didn't win anything – his best position was second in South Africa's Giro del Capo.

He had no major amateur victories behind him, and his progress through the sport was a far cry from some of the bigger names. To put this in some context, Lance Armstrong was already a professional triathlete by the age of 16. He was the US national amateur triathlon champion, and a year after becoming a professional cyclist he won ten times. At the age of 22, Armstrong was the youngest world champion in history.

Miguel Indurain, at the age of 18, was the youngest winner of the Spanish National Amateur Road Championship. At 20 he was the youngest rider to have led the Vuelta a España.

And Eddy Merckx, considered to be the most successful cyclist in history, had already won 80 races as an amateur before he turned professional.

Froome turned professional at the age of 22 – late in the day by modern standards. But he has a physiology that makes his power-to-weight ratio among the best in the sport. He has an incredible endurance capacity. His passion, dedication and ability to push himself to the limit have been the hallmark of his entire career and the driving force behind his progress. And in the 2008 Tour de France, he added self-belief to the mix.

But there was still one ingredient lacking in Chris Froome's cycling and, arguably, he has yet to perfect this: his technical skills on a bicycle have yet to match the other elements of his cycling make-up.

And he also took a long time to perfect the tactical side of bike racing.

Learning the secrets of the trade

'Being a newbie in a pro peloton is a bit like being a student driver on a Los Angeles freeway: move fast, or else.'

Chris Froome has learnt the hard way not to take anything for granted in a bike race.

His biggest lesson in this respect came in South Africa in 2008. Froome was riding in the World's View Challenge in Pietermaritzburg. On the second day, going up one of the climbs, Froome dropped the bunch and was on his own coming to the finish. He had built up a lead of two minutes, and believed this was secure. His radio was faulty, so communication with his team manager, Claudio Corti, was patchy and he wasn't receiving team instructions clearly.

Behind him, Robert Hunter and the sprinters were surging forward. The drop into Pietermaritzburg is quick. As Froome came to the finish, a spectator shouted that he still had a two-minute gap. But he didn't: the gap was now only a few seconds.

Oblivious to this, Froome sat up on his bike, zipped up his jersey, nonchalantly lifted his hands off the bars and prepared to celebrate what he thought was a certain victory. And then all hell broke loose.

Kevin McCallum was in the lead race official's car when it

happened: 'The next thing, the peloton comes flying around the corner towards Chris. His teammate Daryl Impey looks up, sees Chris. Chris looks back, and there's just shock all over his face. It was the funniest thing. They're about 100 metres from the line and there are riders flying past Chris. Behind him riders are crashing and one of them, who swerved to avoid Chris, took out Impey. Afterwards Chris kept saying, "I thought I had two minutes."'

McCallum refers to it as the day Chris Froome learnt in cycling that nothing is won until it is won. Fortunately for Froome, teammate Hunter won the sprint. But Froome took the lesson to heart. 'I feel pretty stupid right now. I thought I had so much time. Someone shouted at me that I had time. That won't happen again,' Froome told McCallum.

Froome was learning lessons from the day he turned professional and until as late as 2011.

When going downhill, he would often use his back brakes. The correct procedure is to grip the front brakes to slow the bike – the rationale being that this is where the bulk of the rider's weight is distributed on the bike during a descent – and the back brakes are used to come to a complete stop. By just gripping the back brakes, the rider makes the bike start to fishtail all over the road.

Another big lesson Froome learnt was how to ride in the bigger pelotons in Europe. The peloton in a cycle race is the whole pack of riders, and it is a hornet's nest of tactics, egos, agendas and, now and then, good-natured fun.

The rider at the front of the peloton bears the brunt of the hard work. He suffers most at the hands of the elements, such as wind. Riders who fall in behind the leader can reduce the wind drag on themselves by up to 40 per cent. This is known as drafting. The aim is to remain as near to the front of the peloton as possible while conserving enough energy to be able to attack at the right time. Breaks made by riders away from the peloton are either legitimate attempts to take the lead or purely a tactical move designed to draw out other key riders in the hopes of tiring them. Much like birds flying in a 'V' formation, a team will position itself at the front of the peloton and rotate its riders to keep them fresh as they work for the star in the team.

Often only inches separate one rider's wheel from another's. The riders rely heavily on instinct and, unable to see too far ahead if they are in the middle or at the back, trust the movements of the peloton and move with it, hoping their brethren up front will not lead them into a crash. When something goes wrong, there are often only seconds to react.

Even the greats have learnt their lessons in the peloton the hard way. Writing for *Cyclingnews*, Greg LeMond recalls racing in the 1982 Liège–Bastogne–Liège road race in his second year as a professional:

Didi Thurau was the big German star at the time, and I was just the young punk, 20 years old. I started at the back, knowing then that you should be either in the front or back of the peloton. If you were in the middle, you'd be in what I called the dead zone – it was that dangerous.

It was raining and the brakes were not that responsive. Out of my right ear, I could hear someone calling, 'Greg, Greg, Greg!' I finally looked over and there was a photographer. I looked back in front of me, then he called me once again and I looked over to give him a smile for the shot.

When I turned back, I saw to my horror that the bunch had come to a near stop. I slammed on the brakes, they didn't respond and I went flying into Didi. He went down heavily, breaking his arm, I went down and broke my collarbone.

In his book, *The Secret Race*, Tyler Hamilton recalls his first experience of the European pelotons: 'Being a newbie in a pro peloton is a bit like being a student driver on a Los Angeles freeway: move fast, or else.'

Riding effectively in a peloton can, at best, secure you victory or, at worst, kill you. The legendary Italian sprinter Mario Cipollini described the internal workings of a professional peloton as 'like a war on the bike, with the words and the mind'.

Froome experienced what most African riders do, and took the giant leap from pelotons in South Africa that were 30 to 40 riders strong, to pelotons in Italy with as many as 150 riders. What makes the European pelotons so much more challenging is that such a large group of cyclists, all vying for position, is squeezed into the narrowest of roads.

The movement of a peloton is similar to a wave as it drifts across the road, and the greatest riders have been able to predict how this happens and when the gaps will form for the briefest of moments, allowing them to slip through closer to the front. Froome had never learnt any of this in his career, and quickly found himself in the deep end in Europe.

Andrew Hood, an American cycling correspondent who has covered every Tour de France since 1996 and has been the European correspondent for *VeloNews* cycling magazine since 2002, has also watched Froome learn the skills required to survive in the European pelotons.

Hood first saw Froome during the 2008 Tour de France. 'I think that's the first time he got on most people's radar in terms of the European racing scene. African riders don't get much attention until they get to Europe, so up until that point nobody had really heard of him. Although Sky say they first noticed him at the 2006 Commonwealth Games.'

Like most, Hood was intrigued by Froome, purely because he was such a rarity as a rider from Africa. But he didn't stand out beyond this. Says Hood:

He seemed like a fish out of water. I saw him as this gangly, skinny kid who was fighting everything. It seemed like he had natural talent, but he was struggling to find his way in the European peloton, which is an animal in itself. A lot of young riders go through this steep learning curve in the pro peloton.

Some guys get their heads around it, and some cannot. You get a lot of riders who have great engines but can't handle the daily tactics and stress of a race. Chris made a lot of mistakes. He would attack at the wrong moments and dig too deep too early on a climb so that when the attack would come he didn't have anything left in the tank to give.

Riding in the bunch is an art. When you're riding in the bunch on flat stretches of road, if you're in a bad position you can burn up a lot of energy just trying to stay in that bunch. It's all about conserving your strength for when you need it.

There is also little patience shown towards rookies:

There's a lot of verbal abuse. Robbie Hunter is one of those guys who'd shout at young riders to get out the way. The top riders swear at the new guys and tell them to get to the back of the bunch because they're worried their inexperience will cause a crash. It takes a couple of years to fight and earn the respect of the peloton, so that when you get up next to a guy like Hunter he knows you, he's heard of you, and he's like, 'Okay, he can be here.' Otherwise, they'll just tell you to get the hell out of there. It's like you haven't earned the right yet to be at the front of the bunch. And it's a lot tougher on the guys coming from Africa, Australia and even the United States. It takes a strong character to survive it, especially if you're doing it yourself like Chris did.

The implication behind Hood's last statement is that knowing one or two stronger or more experienced riders in a peloton – a mentor who is looking out for you when another rider wants to nudge you out of the way or gets too verbal – can make the adaptation that much easier. Being on your own is like arriving for your first day at a new school in your previous school uniform – you're an automatic target and any weakness will be exploited.

* * *

When he joined the Konica Minolta team in 2007, Froome was still very much this kind of raw product learning the skills of his sport. His team enrolled him as a trainee with the Union Cycliste Internationale (UCI) World Cycling Centre (WCC) in Switzerland.

Here they remember him as the 22-year-old with flowing blond hair and two passports – British and Kenyan – and who was completely overwhelmed at riding in a peloton with 200 cyclists.

Alex Roussel was the WCC's head mechanic when Froome was there. Interviewed for an official UCI video and standing in his workshop, with wheels hanging from the ceiling, Roussel is paying meticulous attention to the bicycle in front of him. A soft-spoken, clean-cut individual, Roussel appears every bit the kind of man who deals in details and misses nothing in the pursuit of excellence on the machines he hones for his riders. But, as was the case so many times before, Froome's potential to become a Tour de France champion escaped even his eagle eye. 'Nobody thought his career would turn out like this ... What did stand out was his determination. Arriving from Kenya, he came to find success in cycling, and his sole objective was to turn professional.'

Roussel doesn't recall Froome possessing any outstanding leadership skills, although his calmness under pressure did impress him. He referred to it as a kind of 'British self-control'. He and all of the staff at the WCC were also struck by Froome's pleasant nature and cheerfulness. But he doesn't hesitate to say that in the six years between leaving the WCC and becoming Tour de France champion, Froome has made tremendous strides:

When he was with us, he won a stage of an Italian regional race and won the Mi-Août Bretonne, but he never dominated his category. He did have the potential to become an exceptional rider. On his way to the top he has encountered people who have helped him improve in certain technical areas. He had the qualities of a climber ... But he was also a *rouleur* [all-rounder] and competed in the World Championships time trial. The Mi-Août Bretonne was a good demonstration of his exceptional physical qualities. But he had major technical faults. He has worked hard to correct these while being surrounded by good people throughout his career.

But even his victory in the Mi-Août Bretonne did little to convince the cycling world of his potential. This road race, established in 1960 and held in Brittany, does not have a high position in the UCI European tour ranking in terms of difficulty. It was Froome's only victory of the year, and followed his stage victory in the Giro delle Regioni, the Tour of Japan and his third place overall in the All-Africa Games.

From April to September 2007, Froome soaked up everything he could while he was at the WCC and competing in Italian regional races. Michel Thèze, Froome's coach at the WCC, recalls, 'He wasn't bad. He could do everything. He was aggressive without being nasty about it.'

Slowly, in his own patient way, Froome was showing that he was indeed a special talent. And he was being spotted. While riding for the WCC, Froome made an impression in the 2007 Giro delle Regioni. He finished second in stage 2, came close to winning stage 4 in Tuscany with an impressive breakaway that held off the entire peloton for a long time, and then won stage 5.

Luca Scinto, a former cyclist and then the manager of

the Italian under-23 team, liked what he saw in Froome and made him an offer to join his team after Froome had already committed to Konica Minolta. Although his salary with Konica Minolta was meagre, it was nevertheless cash and he got the exposure he needed to break into the professional arena.

Others were also beginning to see that Froome was a special, if undeveloped, talent.

Claudio Corti certainly thought so. After retiring from professional cycling in 1990, Corti became one of the sport's most respected team managers, and in 2008 the Italian had signed up for this role with Team Barloworld for a third time.

Corti had already developed an interest in Froome, thanks largely to Robert Hunter's persistent attempts to persuade him that Froome was a talent worth investing in. 'I saw him last year [2007] in some races and I could tell he was a good racer,' Corti told *Cyclingnews* in November 2008.

When he signed on with Corti, Froome relocated to Chiari. The town was close enough to Milan, which is where his then girlfriend was working as a model, but when their relationship ended, he moved to the Italian lakeside town of Como.

There was a by now familiar theme discernible in Corti's words in an interview he gave to Italian daily newspaper *Corriere della Sera* in 2008: 'This year, he had his ups and downs, but when he was good, he was flying.'

Froome was thought to have potential, but his ability to deliver consistently was still questionable. It is believed a bilharzia infection he probably contracted in Kenya was largely responsible for this. However, Froome's focus was evident even to Corti: 'He is a serious rider and he has clear ideas.'

Corti recalls an incident in which Froome's determination shone through. 'After a Coppa Ugo Agostoni [a race held in Lissone, northern Italy], Chris insisted he wanted to put miles on his legs. He wanted to cycle home with a backpack. That meant another two hours in the saddle. My problem with it was that miles in the legs should be done at specific times. Certainly not in August and having just finished a few big races. And with a backpack. But it showed his desire to be the best.'

Corti exposed Froome to some top-level European cycling to help him make the step up, and the young rider was suddenly competing against some of the best riders on the planet.

In March 2008, Froome rode in France's Critérium International and finished 45th behind German Jens Voigt. In April he finished 121st in the Gent–Wevelgem race in Belgium. In the same month, Froome finished 139th in the Amstel Gold Race, in the Netherlands, where the starter introduced him as 'the white Kenyan'. He went on to finish 115th in Belgium's La Flèche Wallonne and 84th in the Liège–Bastogne–Liège, another Belgian race.

'I did all the big races ... That was some first year as a neo-pro,' said Froome. 'That was the year my mother passed away, so it was quite a dramatic year ... Also, trying to set up in a new country, learn a new language, it was quite a shock in 2008.'

It was an intense two-month introduction to top-level European cycling, and it was designed to give Corti the affirmation he sought when, at the beginning of the year, he had decided that Froome would race the Tour de France that July.

'I was told at the beginning of the year that riding the Tour was possible – it was not one-hundred per cent ... I went well in the beginning of the season and I showed potential. I only really knew a couple of weeks before; there were a few of us up for the two spots,' Froome told *Cyclingnews* in November 2008.

Froome took everything he could from that first Tour de France. On the Alpe d'Huez, he quickly learnt a lesson in energy balance. During the climb, Corti had called him back to the team car to get more energy gels. 'No. I'm fine,' Froome yelled. He had one more gel in his pocket. Then, about 4 kilometres into the climb, he blew out. 'That hit home how important energy is, that showed me a lesson,' he said.

But he also started to realise his love and talent for the grand tours, and in particular the Tour de France. 'I love the climbs in the Tour. The mountain passes are not like the Italian passes, which are extremely steep, where I start to struggle,' he said at the time.

And the man who seemed to ride up the mountains with ease in 2013 discovered another thing during the 2008 Tour de France. 'The Pyrenees weren't as steep as I expected,' he said. Veteran French journalist Jean-François Quénet was also impressed with Froome's climbing ability on that tour: 'The Kenyan rookie from Barloworld showed pure climbing skills, giving an indication of the bright future he has ...'

Reflecting the feeling within the Barloworld team at the

time, Hood was simply amazed that Froome and these young African riders had survived a tough tour: 'It was impressive for those guys to even get through the tour, and for a rider like Froome to get thrown into his first tour like that, he did really well. It's rare that a first-time tour rider does that well and it showed he had this determination.'

In 2009 Froome continued his solid progress, finishing second to Hunter in the Giro del Capo in South Africa, 36th in the Giro d'Italia and seventh in the Young Riders Classification. That July he returned to South Africa to win the Jock race in Barberton.

It was then that he began to seriously attract the interest of Team Sky. With Sky, Froome honed his skills as a *super-domestique*. But there was still nothing to suggest he was anything more than this.

That all changed during the 2011 Vuelta a España. As Carera puts it, that was 'the big time' for Froome.

The Vuelta

'I just had a fantastic day and somehow I've ended up in the leader's jersey.'

The 2011 Vuelta a España was bound to be a memorable one. It was the first time in 33 years that the race had ventured into the politically volatile Basque region. Alongside the Tour de France and the Giro d'Italia, the Vuelta is the youngest of cycling's three prestigious so-called grand tours.

It was born of the same inspiration as the Tour de France and the Giro d'Italia – namely, to sell newspapers. The Tour de France was aimed at increasing the circulation of its main sponsor, *L'Auto*, and the Giro d'Italia was conceived in the same vein – to promote *La Gazzetta dello Sport*. The Vuelta's main media beneficiary was Spanish daily *Informaciones*.

Other parallels with the other big European races are the fact it was also considered a brutal test of human endurance, and, consequently, riders used to resort to consuming all manner of cocktails to boost their performances, one of which was a mixture of gin, vermouth and bitters.

The Vuelta is unfairly considered to be inferior to the other grand tours. And it is the only one of the three races not to have had a home winner on its debut: Belgian Gustaaf Deloor took the inaugural honours in 1935.

In some ways, the status of the Vuelta mirrors the general perception of Spanish cycling for many years. It is a tour with a history that is intertwined with the Spanish Civil War and then the dictatorial regime of General Franco – a Spain that was literally starving and mired in an economic recession brought on by the Franco regime.

Even as recently as the 1980s, foreign cyclists were shocked by the conditions they had to endure while competing in Spain. In his autobiography, *We Were Young and Carefree*, Laurent Fignon describes his experience of the Vuelta in 1983:

Everyone has forgotten what it was like back then. Spain had only just emerged from the Franco era. It was like the Third World; anyone who went over there at the start of the

1980s would know what I mean. For cyclists like us, the accommodation and the way we were looked after were not easy to deal with. Sometimes it was barely acceptable. Professional cyclists of today cannot imagine what it was like in the 1980s in a hotel in the backside of beyond in Asturias or the Pyrenees. The food was rubbish and sometimes there was no hot water, morning or evening.

Spanish cyclists were not highly regarded among their peers – a sentiment that even found its way into literature. In Ernest Hemingway's *The Sun Also Rises*, Hemingway's character Jake meets a group of French and Belgian cyclists riding in the Tour du Pays Basque. 'The Spaniards, they said, did not know how to pedal,' Hemingway wrote.

However, in the 1950s Spanish cycling began to come into its own. And it was in the Basque country that it flourished, experiencing a revival in 1955 to the point that the Vuelta has been held annually ever since.

Today, the youngest sibling of the grand tours has some notable achievements to its name, such as the smallest margin of victory in any grand tour – the six seconds by which Frenchman Éric Caritoux beat Spaniard Alberto Fernández in 1984. The Tour de France's smallest margin of victory is eight seconds, which occurred in the 1989 triumph by Greg LeMond over Laurent Fignon. And the Giro d'Italia's is 11 seconds, the time by which Fiorenzo Magni beat Ezio Cecchi in 1948.

But, in the same way that the Spanish can be tempestuous, the Vuelta has also had its stormy moments. Most notably, it was the first of the grand tours to have its winner stripped of his title because of doping. That ignominy befell Angel Arroyo in 1982.

Then there was the tragedy of Ireland's Shay Elliott. A year after Tom Simpson became the first British rider to have worn the yellow jersey in the Tour de France, Elliott matched the feat for Ireland. He went on to become the first English-speaking rider to win stages in all three of the grand tours. But, as uncovered by Lucy Fallon and Adrian Bell in their book *Viva La Vuelta! – The Story of Spain's Great Bike Race*, Elliott's victory in the fourth stage of the 1962 Vuelta a España had a tragic consequence. His prize for winning the stage was a shotgun. And it was this gun that brought an end to one of the great stories in cycling. On 4 May 1971, Elliott was found dead in his home in Dublin from a self-inflicted shotgun wound. His marriage and business interests had failed, and his father had passed away two weeks before.

But, in 2011, the drama of the Vuelta was of a different nature. This time, two riders who were meant to be the *domestiques* for their team leaders ended up dominating in Spain.

For Froome in particular, his performance in the Vuelta would be the catalyst to see him start becoming a major force in the grand tours. After his second-place finish in the 2011 Vuelta, he finished second in the 2012 Tour de France, fourth in the 2012 Vuelta and then first in the 2013 Tour de France.

Froome came into the 2011 Vuelta as the *domestique* for Bradley Wiggins. In the Spanish-based team Geox-TMC, Juan José Cobo was the *domestique* for Russian Denis Menchov. Neither were meant to win the Vuelta – not Froome, a solid

Amid the shacks in a village outside Nairobi, David Kinjah taught Chris Froome everything he knew about bicycles and cycling. GALLO IMAGES/AFP

Kinjah's Safari Simbaz watch as the greatest cyclist ever to hail from their ramshackle club wins the 2013 Tour de France. GALLO IMAGES/AFP

Clive Froome once questioned his son's singular focus on cycling; Chris went from a young boy who would push himself to the point of exhaustion to Tour de France champion. GALLO IMAGES/FOTO24 /MARY-ANN PALME

Froome (second row from back, third from right) was a house prefect at St John's College, Houghton. BY KIND COURTESY OF ST JOHN'S COLLEGE

Riding for Team Barloworld in 2008, Froome was given his first taste of just how tough the Tour de France can be. GALLO IMAGES/AFP

With Team Sky, Froome found his niche in an environment where a premium is placed on attention to detail. BRYN LENNON/GETTY IMAGES/GALLO IMAGES

Lance Armstrong: The doping saga has left a cloud of conspiracy over cycling that has often driven a wedge between the cyclists, their fans and the media. AAI/FOTOSTOCK

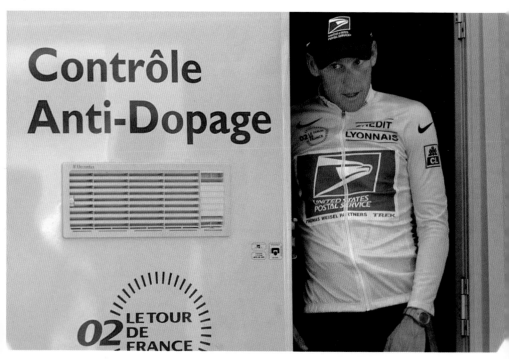

Mont Ventoux is a barren, mountain finish that has been likened to cycling hell.
AAI/FOTOSTOCK

Froome's dominant ride up Mont Ventoux was one of the greatest in the history of cycling, but exposed him to a barrage of questions about doping.
AAI/FOTOSTOCK

The art of riding in a massive peloton on narrow European roads is something Chris Froome had to learn quickly. GREATSTOCK/CORBIS

As team leader of Barloworld, Robbie Hunter became the first South African to win a stage in the Tour de France – he won stage 11 in 2007. INPRA

Froome's break came in the 2011 Vuelta a España. He finished on the podium, which took him from a rider Team Sky were considering dropping to a cyclist they could hone into a Tour de France champion. GREATSTOCK/CORBIS

rider but dogged by technical inconsistencies and fighting for his survival within Team Sky, nor Cobo, the man who only a few months earlier had been ready to quit cycling and become an electrician.

Yet both utterly overshadowed the men they were meant to be helping to victory. Froome had already piqued the interest of the European teams, and French outfit Cofidis was among the first big teams to come calling. This was the team that had taken on Lance Armstrong, before releasing him because of his cancer, and David Millar, a former British national road-cycling champion and a multiple stage winner in the grand tours. Unfortunately, both have since been involved in highly publicised doping scandals.

'About 25 days before the Vuelta, we had a proposal from Cofidis,' recalls Carera. 'Chris wanted to sign because he wasn't sure what was happening with Sky.'

Sky were equally unsure about Froome. They seemed to have the same perception of him as the author and cycling journalist Chris Sidwells, who recalls his experience of Froome as

a fantastic cycling talent, but as hapless and scatter-brained if very likeable an individual as you could ever wish to meet. So scatter-brained that in turning this uncut diamond into the jewel he is now, even Team Sky nearly gave up in exasperation.

Halfway through his first year with the team, one of their staff told me that they were at a loss as to what to do with him. He clearly had the ability but he made mistakes. Okay, fair enough, everybody makes them, but even after having an error pointed out to him as forcibly as possible, Froome went ahead and did it again.

Sidwells, like those at Team Sky, didn't see much of a future beyond this for Froome: 'His future with Sky looked bleak ... Sky seriously considered letting him go at the end of 2011. Then the Vuelta happened.'

Despite Froome's desire to sign for Cofidis, Carera advised him against it. 'Before the start of the Vuelta, I said to Chris, "How do you think you will do?" He says to me, "I think I can ride a very good Vuelta." So I told him we would wait another two weeks before signing anything. "First you work hard for Wiggins."'

And then the grand plan changed again. Froome rewrote the script on the ninth day of the race.

As James Callow wrote in the *Guardian*, 'The stage had been set for Bradley Wiggins, the three-time Olympic champion and figurehead of Team Sky, to become only the fifth Briton to lead the Vuelta a España.'

Instead, it was Froome who took the red jersey when he finished second in the individual time trial and took the general classification lead by 12 seconds.

'I wasn't really expecting that,' Froome told Callow. 'I was just trying to stay in contention and be there along with Bradley Wiggins, the team leader. I just had a fantastic day and somehow I've ended up in the leader's jersey.'

As Froome stood there on the podium, almost blushing at having upstaged his team leader, Carera's phone started ringing. 'During that day, we had six proposals for his services,' says Carera.

One of those hunting Froome was the eccentric Jonathan Vaughters of Team Garmin. 'We started to talk to him five or six days into the Vuelta, before he'd done anything incredible but as his performance got better and better, he just became out of reach financially. It just became unrealistic for me to continue down that path. I offered him a contract but as soon as he started doing well at the Vuelta ... it was just a case of being a day late and a dollar short,' Vaughters revealed.

Cycling correspondent Andrew Hood recalls the surprise at Froome's performance:

> He caught a lot of people by surprise in terms of where he came from so quickly. In the 2007 season, he won a few races in Europe. When he came to Italy he won one or two races right from the start. They were mountain-top finishes. To win anything in Italy is pretty telling, especially on a mountain. You've got to be pretty damn good.
>
> But being in those small teams, it's hard to show yourself with a result. It takes a couple of years to get into the groove at this level. His trajectory was definitely not normal. So when it came to the 2011 Vuelta, other riders in the peloton were literally asking the question, where did this guy Froome come from?

As the interest in Froome grew, once again the wily Carera advised his client to wait. 'I talked with Chris and we decided to wait until the last day before signing anything, because now he had a chance to finish on the podium. But, that day, when he took the red jersey, that was the day his life changed forever.'

Froome's transformation had caught even his own team by surprise. As mentioned, he was originally given the role of *domestique* to protect Wiggins, who was coming back from a broken collarbone he had sustained in the 2011 Tour de France, but then Sky suddenly woke up to Froome's true potential. They released him from the shackles of being Wiggins's 'servant', and Froome responded as he chased down the leader, Cobo. Their battle came to a head during the final mountaintop finish on stage 17, from Faustino V to Peña Cabarga.

Froome started the stage second in the general classification behind Cobo. Several groups had tried to escape early in the stage, but had all been brought back by the time they reached the final climb.

At 6 kilometres, it's a short, explosive climb, and it provided all the fireworks for a memorable stage. Exactly on the final kilometre mark, Cobo made his attack. But Froome stayed with him, and only a few metres later he accelerated past the Spaniard. Froome kept up a strong pace, with Cobo falling off for a while before responding again, surging past Froome.

Froome stayed on his wheel, and accelerated past Cobo on the inside of the last bend to take the win and reduce Cobo's overall lead to only 13 seconds. Both riders were exhausted after what Froome described as 'one of the hardest days on the bicycle of my life'.

It was another monumental effort from Froome, and another powerful reminder of his climbing strength.

In the end, however, Froome and Team Sky ran out of race time to catch up with Cobo overall. But the second-place finish was a career-changer for Froome.

★ ★ ★

When Froome started in the 2011 Vuelta, Carera confirmed that he was on a contract of €100 000 a year. At the end of the race, Sky put a new contract in front of the man they had recently considered offloading. 'It was ten times more,' says Carera. Now, Carera told Froome, they could finally sign. Froome put his name to a new three-year contract with Sky. 'After the race, Chris and his father and I went to the Vuelta party. Sky was the perfect team for his great goal – the Tour de France. That night at the party, Chris understood. He understood his life had changed. He knew it.'

Hood believes few teams, if any, could have tapped Froome's potential in the way Sky has done:

> Chris signing with Team Sky was fundamental to his rise. I don't think any other team would've done this for him. It was really key to his development. I think with any other team he would've been lost. Sky have very intense and sci-entific training programmes for their riders. They have very specific training in terms of improving their high-end power. They train with these seven-hour efforts and finish with an attack, just like an actual stage. And they do this day after day after day. Other teams aren't training at their level. The environment at Sky also suits Chris. Bradley Wiggins said Chris Froome was the perfect rider for Sky because he's quiet, dedicated, professional and ambitious, and gives everything. He needed the clear direction Sky gave him. He needed somebody to tap that potential.

But there was also something inside Froome that needed to come out, in a very literal sense.

Bilharzia

'I take heavy medication to suppress the disease, but when you are diagnosed with bilharzia you never lose it.'

Bilharzia has been cited as the reason behind Froome's inconsistency throughout his career.

Bilharzia (or schistosomiasis, to give it its medical name, also known as snail fever) is a parasitic disease. Its life cycle begins with eggs that become parasitic worms, which later develop into a swimming version, which is the point where humans become infected. But for this to take place, the parasite needs freshwater snails as a host. Once waterborne, the parasite makes contact with human skin and then burrows into the blood vessels, making its way to the liver, a major supply of blood. It then lays eggs.

Most of the parasites gather around the gut and bladder. Testing for the parasite eggs is done in the stool and urine. Because it has various life cycles and can travel around the body, bilharzia can manifest in various ways. The most obvious and immediate symptom is a rash. The body reacts to the parasite by activating the immune system, which can bring on the symptoms of a dramatic fever (called Katayama's fever) and extreme tiredness. If the disease is untreated, the symptoms can become more chronic, depending on where the eggs are located.

Froome says that he only discovered he had bilharzia in 2010, which would have made him 25 at the time. 'I was at my brother's wedding in Kenya in late 2010 when the

International Cycling Union checked my blood passport. I immediately asked for all parameters when they discovered that I suffered from the disease. That was why I was sometimes abnormally tired and was just average with Team Barloworld and my first year at Sky. These tiny worms affect your whole organism.'

It is almost certain that Froome contracted the disease as a child in Kenya, having lived an outdoor life there. His brother Jeremy told *The Telegraph* how they used to collect snakes, fish in dams and shoot ducks in rice paddies. The writer of the article, Ian Chadband, adds: 'Those fields were riddled with bilharzia, the debilitating parasitic infection which affected all three brothers for years and which seriously stunted Chris's first years as a professional.'

The worms feed on the red blood cells in the body, which for an endurance athlete is a nightmare, as these cells are principally responsible for carrying oxygen in the body. As Froome said, 'The disease just drained my immune system. I was always getting little colds and coughs, nothing serious, but it always kept me from being at 100 per cent fitness.'

Leading South African sports physician Dr Jon Patricios suggests that Froome's ability to compete at a high level despite the bilharzia is impressive, though not impossible: 'At the level these athletes are training, even the smallest discrepancy in their health is a problem in terms of causing fatigue and a decrease in performance. This is an infection, and the body has to expend energy to fight any infection.'

But Froome's case is not as rare as might be thought or as has been portrayed. Though he has never had first-hand experience of a bilharzia patient, Patricios says there are several documented cases of elite sportspeople competing while infected with the parasite. The most notable cases are endurance athletes from Kenya and Ethiopia.

'It's quite well described in textbooks, particularly in the East African athletes. As an African condition, it's not uncommon. It probably just appears unlikely in Froome because he's essentially a First World athlete from a Third world environment.'

This probably explains Froome's misdiagnosis for so many years. Bilharzia is second only to malaria in terms of the most common diseases caused by parasites. About 85 per cent of the global cases occur in sub-Saharan Africa, and 40 per cent of the Kenyan population is affected by it. Such high infection rates place it firmly on the radar of most medical professionals in Africa, along with malaria. However, if Froome was being treated in Europe, it is highly likely not to have been picked up, as the disease is uncommon there.

It's one of those great ironies that, if Froome had remained in the Kenyan environment, they would have picked it up earlier. After the bilharzia was diagnosed in 2010, Froome said, 'I've been receiving treatment for two years now. For the first half of the year, I take heavy medication to suppress the disease, but when you are diagnosed with bilharzia you never lose it.'

In July 2013, Froome told *VeloNews* writer Andrew Hood, 'I do go for a check-up every six months. The last was in January and it was still in my system. I take Biltricide. It kills the parasite in the system.'

The treatment for bilharzia is straightforward. It usually

requires only a single dose of the tablet, administered according to body weight, to destroy the parasite. No more than three or four treatments should be required. However, the eggs are much harder to eradicate and can remain in the body for years.

Biltricide (generic name praziquantel) is not included in the World Anti-Doping Agency's banned-substances list and does not require a therapeutic-use exemption (TUE). 'It's a very strong pill,' says Froome. 'It basically kills everything in your system, and hopefully at the same time, kills the parasite ... You cannot train when you're taking that. The treatment is pretty rough stuff. There was more than a week when I could not even touch the bike.'

During the 2013 Tour de France, Froome said he did not have a TUE for bilharzia treatment.

'TUEs are a rather personal issue, but I am able to say I do not have any TUEs during this tour. Hopefully I will not have any.'

TUEs have been viewed with suspicion during the tour's doping era because they have been used as loopholes for doctors to prescribe banned substances for cyclists. The UCI rules permit cyclists to use certain substances if they can back it up with a doctor's prescription. For example, if a cyclist has a legitimate ailment such as a saddle sore, he can get a TUE allowing him to use cortisone treatment. But, during the doping era, doctors were using this as a means of prescribing illegal drugs for riders.

According to Hood, 'none of the Team Sky riders had TUEs during the 2013 Tour de France. TUEs have always been seen as a back door to cutting corners. About six years ago, there were 80 to 90 riders in the tour that had TUEs for asthma. How can 90 asthmatics compete in the Tour de France? Team Sky wanted to make a big statement by not having any TUEs.'

In a heated exchange in the cycling forum Velorooms with some commentators who were sceptical about Froome's bilharzia treatment, Froome's fiancée, Michelle Cound, to whom he had become engaged in March 2013, wrote: 'If you're that interested, the medication is a strong anti-parasitic called Prazitel. He took it at the end of March after Critérium International; he had also taken two courses of praziquantel in the past but the parasites kept coming back. He was diagnosed back in 2010, if I remember correctly. It's difficult to say when it was contracted.'

Responding to a statement that bilharzia treatment was similar to chemotherapy, Cound wrote, 'I don't know where you got that rubbish ... I was with Chris when he took the 7-day (NOT 6-week) course of medication (immediately following Critérium International) and while there was some mild nausea and fatigue, it certainly wasn't anything like a chemo treatment. He obviously wasn't able to ride while taking the medication. And, yes, he definitely has been struggling with bilharzia ... he is due for another test to see if it's cleared his system. Really ... get your facts straight before making accusations like that ... pathetic.'

For the Team Sky principal, David Brailsford, the bilharzia was a perfect explanation for Froome's inconsistency. And for many others, the diagnosis and treatment have explained Froome's sudden rise from just a professional to grand tour contender.

'There was an inconsistency about him,' Brailsford says. 'The question wasn't why he was good, the question was why we'd only seen glimpses. Why isn't he like that all the time? When the illness was discovered, retrospectively, it made a lot of sense. There would be certain stages in the front group, you'd see these glimpses, but he couldn't put it together with some consistency.'

Comments made by Froome and Team Sky over the last few years would also appear to support the influence of the infection. In 2010, speaking ahead of the Giro d'Italia, Brailsford was quoted on the Team Sky website as saying that Chris had been ill and was also coming back from a crash so they wanted to nurse him back and make sure he was ready to go.

In August that year, Froome tweeted: 'That's the last time I get sick this year!! Back with a vengeance now ...'

In May 2011, a few months before his breakthrough in the Vuelta, a Sky article previewing the Tour of California stated, 'Froome proved there are few stronger after an impressive run to 15th overall at the Tour de Romandie at the end of April, yet the Kenyan-born rider has seen his preparations take a knock following a chest infection.'

Froome went on to explain: 'When I got back from Romandie, I had to take about a week off the bike because I got a bit of a chest infection and cough. That held me back a little bit ...'

His coach, Bobby Julich, also confirmed that 'in the 2011 Tour of California, he was amazing one day and really bad the next. So we tested for bilharzia again and, sure enough, he had it. And, once he got treatment, he started progressing again.'

Shortly before the Vuelta, Froome was quoted on the Team Sky website as saying, 'I've had one or two problems with illness but we've treated them and the team have been really supportive. They are sorted and, touch wood, everything seems to be going in the right direction right now.'

Julich (who in October 2012 was asked to leave Team Sky after admitting having taken a banned substance during his own racing career in the 90s when he was a teammate of Lance Armstrong) says, 'We did some lab testing with him early in the year and it wasn't making sense. I saw the numbers and said that the machines must be calibrated wrong, because these were the numbers of a guy who would finish on the Tour de France podium. I was told, no, they were right. I was amazed.'

In March 2012, Froome's inconsistency was again apparent. He was diagnosed with bilharzia once again and forced to take the required medication for a week after the Critérium International, as explained by Cound in the Velorooms cycling forum.

Team Sky say that they continue to monitor Froome's bilharzia and treat it accordingly. The disease, coupled with Froome's technical inefficiencies, makes for a highly plausible explanation as to his sudden rise amid often erratic performances. Julich links the two when he says:

> But when we started working together, I realised straight away that Chris needed some work on organisation and structure. He was a real tinkerer – always changing his shoes, his training, his diet or whatever. He had also continued to train too much even when he was suffering with the parasite,

which had knocked his confidence as well as his energy levels. Beyond that, it was all very basic stuff ... Chris did not know how to race. I needed to teach him how to get the watts out at the right time.

5

Master and servant

It is one of the most iconic photographs in sport: the image
of the winner of the Tour de France crossing the finishing
line, wearing the famous yellow jersey and raising his arms
in triumph.

On Sunday 22 July 2012, Bradley Wiggins became the
next subject of this celebrated line of photographs. Wiggins
had made history by becoming the first Briton to win the
Tour de France.

But in the photograph of Wiggins crossing the finishing
line in Paris and raising his arms, the man behind him
now tells the greatest story. Chris Froome, head bowed
and riding in the shadow of Wiggins, took second place in
a tour he could have won, and which many feel he should
have won. But this was not his time. The title of Wiggins's
autobiography, *My Time*, points to Team Sky's decision to
position the eccentric Englishman as their lead rider for the

2012 Tour de France. For Wiggins, this was his time. Froome would have to be content with his role as *super-domestique*. As the servant, he was not there to win – only to help. This relationship is part of the age-old story of competitive cycling, one that has come about in the fragile world of an individual sport run on a team basis.

Teams decide who their best chance at a tour victory is and they put all their efforts into making sure that cyclist wins. All the other riders in the team are there to protect him, help him and ensure that he crosses the finishing line first. Their own interests, goals, ambitions and desires are completely secondary.

But, of course, it doesn't always work out as planned.

One of the most notorious rivalries witnessed in cycling was the Italian pairing of Fausto Coppi and Gino Bartali in the 40s and early 50s. It was a rivalry that even split Italy, with fans dividing themselves along the lines of being *coppiani* or *bartaliani*. Bartali was the hero of the more traditional Italians, while Coppi appealed to the new generation. Bartali was conservative and religious, and even had the support of the Vatican. Coppi was the hero of Italy's industrial north, and his nickname was Fausto the Sinner (because he was living with a married woman to whom he was not married). It is a debate that still rages among Italian cycling fans to this day – who was the better of the two?

Coppi won the Giro d'Italia five times and the Tour de France twice. Bartali won the Giro d'Italia three times and the Tour de France once, with his career interrupted by World War II.

In 1940, the younger Coppi and Bartali became teammates.

Coppi's job was to help Bartali win the Giro d'Italia that year. Instead, Coppi outrode his teammate to victory. And so began their feud. The rivalry reached its nadir in the 1949 World Championships when, rather than work together for the Italian team, they refused to cooperate and quit the race.

They remained bitter rivals, to the extent that even a photograph from the 1952 tour became a long-standing argument between the two. The photo shows Coppi holding a water bottle. Bartali also has his hands on the bottle. Coppi claims he was giving the bottle to Bartali; Bartali claims he was passing it to Coppi. This black-and-white photograph hangs in the home of Coppi's son, Faustino, who, even today declares, 'It was my dad that passed it, not the other way.'

The photograph was taken by Carlo Martini. In an interview in the Italian press, Vito Liverani, considered the grand master of Italian photography, says he knows who passed the bottle. 'But I will not say who passed it to whom – never,' he said.

The Italian rivalry set the tone for some of cycling's most famous feuds. Take the case of Stephen Roche and Roberto Visentini. They had agreed that Roche would support Visentini in his bid to win the 1987 Giro d'Italia, and Visentini would then reciprocate by helping Roche win the Tour de France. But Roche is said to have doubted that Visentini would stick to their agreement, so he rode the 1987 Giro as if to win it himself. They rode the entire race fighting each other, and Roche eventually won.

In the 1986 Tour de France, Greg LeMond, considered one of the gentlemen of cycling, was involved in a feud with his teammate Bernard Hinault. After winning the 1985 tour, Hinault promised LeMond he would help him win the following year. But there was doubt throughout the 1986 tour as to whether Hinault was helping or trying to win it for himself. Eventually, LeMond won.

So it is hardly surprising that there should be some tensions between two star riders from the same team. And this was the case with Wiggins and Froome in the 2012 Tour de France.

But this tension actually stretches further back, to the 2011 Vuelta a España, when Froome and Wiggins roomed together. During that race, the cracks were already evident. Wiggins led early in the race, and many believed Froome was being held back by Team Sky. Froome finished second in the stage 10 time trial and claimed the overall race lead as a result. But, the following day, Froome was back in his supporting role for Wiggins, who reclaimed the red jersey from him.

However, Wiggins faded in the final week of the race, and Froome seemed to grow stronger, eventually finishing second. Had he been given the freedom to attack earlier – and the support of his team – Froome may well have won the Vuelta that year.

Even though Froome's performance in the Vuelta was astounding and secured him his place within Team Sky, Wiggins was still the team's man to lead in the 2012 Tour de France. This despite the fact that during the 2011 Vuelta, Wiggins even suggested to Sky that he should be riding for Froome during that race, as he recalls in his autobiography:

I even asked the team at one point whether I should ride for Chris. And they said I shouldn't, because they were not confident Chris could last the distance. Up to that point Froomie had never done anything like this before, so there was no reason to believe he could sustain it. Even Chris was surprised: he'd been so inconsistent with his performances before then, thanks to the bilharzia parasite that had affected his health. So I guess I was the safer bet for the team. It was a difficult call.

But the tension between the two was building, and came to a head in stage 11 of the 2012 Tour de France. Leading the tour, Wiggins faced an unexpected, and unplanned, attack from Froome about 4 kilometres from the end of the stage to the ski station of La Toussuire. Froome accelerated past Wiggins, but was later called back by the team's sporting director, Sean Yates.

In an interview with *The Times*, Froome explained the much-criticised move:

> I put in an acceleration for 5 or 6 km before the final climb, but as soon as I heard that Brad was in difficulty and he was struggling to stay with the guys I backed off completely. I knew that the correct thing to do would be to stay with Brad and look after him until the finish. He was only a few seconds back so I eased off, let him catch up to me again and escorted him to the finish line. So it just meant that I rode at his pace as opposed to the pace that I felt I could go if I was to try and get that advantage on the other guys.

Froome was lying third in the tour at that point, and argues that his move was simply a means of securing second place overall and ensuring that Sky still had the best possible chance of a victory should Wiggins fail for any reason.

But Wiggins was dumbfounded. Yates, who left the team in light of Sky's zero-tolerance approach to doping and questions surrounding Yates's previous involvement with the teams of dopers Lance Armstrong and Bjarne Riis, later revealed in his book, *It's All About the Bike*, that Wiggins was close to quitting the tour after this incident. According to Yates, he received a text message from Wiggins saying, 'I think it would be better for everyone if I went home.'

Yates writes:

[Wiggins] was upset and felt like Froomey had stabbed him in the back after the discussion we'd had before the stage [where it had been agreed Froome would attack only in the last 500 metres]. He couldn't understand why he'd gone back on the agreement, especially when everything was going so well. There were only four kilometres left at that point and Brad went on to win by three minutes, so the maths say that he would still have been comfortably on top in Paris. However, his mental state was always fragile, and that psychological blow could have been a knockout one.

In his autobiography, Wiggins reveals just how much Froome's move affected him:

It was a really confusing episode. I remember thinking at the finish, 'What the hell was that all about?' ... It was a little bit like having a battle plan going into a war, all being in a trench together, firing your guns at the enemy, and then one of your troops going off and doing his own thing some-where else in another trench, completely unprompted, unplanned, and contrary to your original plan ... I was in the yellow jersey and the hierarchy in the team ... dictates that you have to put your aspirations aside to defend the jersey. That's how it works.

Froome clearly felt that having two strong riders placed well enough in the tour ensured the best possible result for the team. In other words, if Wiggins was first, there was no harm climbing into second behind him just in case he crashed or some other unforeseen event threatened his position at the front. A different view, however, is that when confronted by a rider who had clearly outperformed him in the 2011 Vuelta and was now showing he was stronger than him in this tour, Wiggins's thoughts were drifting to the threat that his own teammate posed.

'From that point on it felt as if we were defending both positions, and if it ever came down to it, if we got exposed, if we were attacked left, right and centre, it would be every man for himself. I never liked being in that position. I felt I was as much under attack from my own teammate as from anybody else,' Wiggins says of the incident. 'I'm leading by two minutes – and all of a sudden my own teammate's attacking ... that shouldn't be at the detriment of the job we're trying to do for me.'

Wiggins felt the strategy had been conclusively decided on the team bus that morning. Froome had indicated his desire to attack and was told by team management that the priority was Wiggins and the yellow jersey. Wiggins recalls that Froome was happy with that decision, but may have been carried away by the heat of the moment. The uncertainty created by this event meant Wiggins was ready to abandon the 2012 tour.

'The problem was that, from that moment on, through the rest of the Tour, I didn't quite know what to expect from Chris when it got into the heat of battle,' says Wiggins. 'When you're in that situation you need cool heads all around you. I felt at any moment he might go off on a tangent to what we had planned earlier in the day; I became very wary.'

The second critical moment came during stage 17. With only a seven-man bunch remaining on this stage in the Pyrenees – both Froome and Wiggins among them – Froome surged ahead of his teammate and made frequent glances back at Wiggins. Some interpreted this as Froome spurring Wiggins on; others saw it as Froome signalling to Wiggins who the stronger of the two was. Wiggins says his perceived weakness at the time was a brief loss of concentration, with thoughts starting to enter his mind that he had won the tour. He says he and Froome had a conversation during the stage, in which Froome indicated he wanted to attack to keep resisting the threat posed by Vincenzo Nibali, who went on to finish third in the tour. Wiggins said he told Froome there was no need for it.

Again, Froome takes the high road when he was criticised for the move:

I didn't leave Brad at all. He started losing my wheel a bit, but every time he'd lose my wheel I'd ease up and let him get back on. That was nothing to do with Bradley physically not keeping up with me. All his big contenders had dropped off, we had got rid of everybody and his mindset was just to keep going and finish the stage and the job. My mindset was to chase Alejandro Valverde up the road to try and win the stage. I felt it was a missed opportunity but I also know you can get too greedy. We were first and second in GC [general classification] and perhaps I was too ambitious, but that's all.

Wiggins is more outspoken about the second incident. 'It felt as if Chris was doing his own thing but I had to deal with it because as the race leader I was the one who was up for scrutiny in front of the press and television every day. The questions I was asking myself about Froomie, and the questions I was being asked each day after the stage finished, certainly didn't make the Tour enjoyable.'

Froome has said the rivalry between him and Wiggins is nothing more than media sensationalism. 'We are not friends. But we've got a good relationship and we've got no problem getting on with each other.'

But the fact that Wiggins devoted eight pages to the topic in his book suggests otherwise. The feud even boiled over to their partners, with Wiggins's wife, Catherine, and Froome's fiancée, Michelle Cound, involved in a furious Twitter spat over Froome's questionable loyalty on that tour.

'Team work is also about giving the people around you, that support you, a chance to shine in their own right,' wrote Cound.

Catherine Wiggins responded with praise for the 'selfless effort and true professionalism' of the other members of the team, omitting to mention Froome.

Cound again took offence, tweeting, 'Typical!' Then she added, 'Don't think there are many other pro riders whose partners know more about cycling than Chris's precisely & I know what happened just then.'

In another tweet, she wrote: 'If you want loyalty, get a Froome dog, a quality I value, although being taken advantage of by others.'

In a subsequent interview in the official guide for the 2013 Tour de France, Cound attempted to set the record straight on her outbursts. 'I was quite vocal about Chris, but I am Chris's biggest fan and obviously I wanted him to perform to the best of his abilities. My intention wasn't to criticise the team: I was caught up in the moment and any tweets I made certainly weren't a reflection of what Chris was thinking. I have strong opinions, those opinions are 100 per cent my own, and Chris doesn't always agree with them.'

Both Froome and Wiggins were at pains to play down any talk of a feud or rivalry, but it clearly existed – certainly in the mind of cycling correspondent Andrew Hood. 'There was definitely tension there. You can only have one sheriff in town, and both of them were big stars and wanted to win. The 2012 Tour was perfectly set up for Wiggins, but Froome had a chance to win as well. Froome was definitely racing his own race.'

Froome revealed in an interview with *L'Équipe* magazine during the 2012 tour the frustration he had, knowing he was good enough to win that Tour de France but that Wiggins was the man for Sky that year. 'This is a very, very large sacrifice,' Froome said. 'I know that I can win this Tour – but not with Sky. We made our plans around Wiggins and everyone respects that. That is difficult because you don't often have the chance in life to win a Tour. But that is my job ... Being the first Briton to win the Tour could change my life. That is why it is such a large sacrifice.'

The issue continued to simmer in the build-up to the 2013 Tour de France, with uncertainty as to which of the two would lead Team Sky. Wiggins came out saying he would love to challenge again and that they might both lead the team in the first week of the tour until the racing decided who was the stronger. But Froome hit back saying he was the team's clear leader for the 2013 Tour. In April, he even issued a personal statement on the matter, which read:

There has been much speculation regarding the leadership for Team Sky at the Tour de France this year. I have made it clear that winning the Tour would be my main objective for 2013. I have been reassured by the management at Team Sky that I have their full backing, and at no time has the leadership of the Tour team been in question. Attempting to win the Tour de France is a massive undertaking, and will take total commitment from each and every team member. The Tour team has yet to be selected but with the depth of talent that we have at Team Sky, I have no doubt that the strongest and most willing riders will be there to support me.

Confidence is high in the camp following the success at the Tour of Romandie. This week I will be doing a recon of the Mont Ventoux summit finish, which could be a critical stage of this year's Tour de France. A group of us will be going to Tenerife next week to continue training at altitude in our build-up to the Tour.

The Team Sky principal, David Brailsford, was quite happy to let both his strongest riders posture in public while he enjoyed the enviable position of having two good candidates for the team's leadership.

In 2010 Brailsford and Shane Sutton had begun the process of building on their success with British Cycling and forming a British team with the stated goal of winning the Tour de France within five years. They would do it clean, and with a British rider on the podium in Paris. It was bold, but Brailsford, then the performance director at British Cycling, and Sutton, the head coach, felt it wasn't that far-fetched. It has a whiff of the same national drive behind the formation of US Postal around Lance Armstrong and the focus to build an American team capable of winning the Tour de France in the 1990s.

Brailsford and Sutton aimed to bring the same levels of professionalism in British Cycling to a tour team, namely, as Wiggins described it, 'a constant search for perfection: the best equipment, the best back-up staff, the best experts to research every area from diet to aerodynamics'.

Brailsford has since repeatedly made the point that he doesn't really care whether Wiggins and Froome get along or not, and that harmony of personalities is not what you are seeking in a high-pressure environment such as the Tour de France, but rather goal harmony.

The whole issue has been ripe for conspiracy theories, one of which is that Wiggins was made the team leader in 2012 because he was 'more British' than Froome, the outsider from one of the 'colonies', and, as such, his victory would have more impact in a year in which Britain was hosting the Olympics.

There is also the belief that the team found it easier to ride for Froome in 2013 than Wiggins in 2012. Wiggins is considered a much more complex character who doesn't share too much with his teammates. He's very much an individual, and he was bound to clash with Froome.

Putting the two riders together in the same team created the perfect storm in terms of their different personalities. But, while Froome has often been described as the nicest man to ever climb into the saddle, the reality is that something definitely changes in him when he is in that saddle.

His ex-teammate at Barloworld, Robbie Hunter, chuckles when I put this to him. 'Chris also puts on a really great face. He won't always stand back just because he's a nice guy. He's very determined and he's selfish to the point that he'll do what's good for him. You have to be selfish to get ahead. Chris knows he's got something to give and he needs to be selfish about it.'

But the most obvious conclusion as to Froome's selection to lead the 2013 tour was the route, which was more mountainous and therefore suited his cycling style.

One theory that was certainly laid to rest was that the Froome–Wiggins rivalry was merely something to drum up publicity. Cound herself denied this on her active Twitter account. 'To those claiming that this Wiggins/Froome thing is some sort of publicity stunt, you are wrong,' she tweeted on 30 April.

She followed this with, 'Chris & Brad on the same start line, in the same kit? Mmmmmm ... doubt it!'

And then she added, 'I look forward to @TeamSky clearing up this mess (ASAP). #fedup'.

Ultimately, the decision was made easier when Wiggins was forced to withdraw from the tour because of injury. Even then, however, there was talk that the injury was not serious enough to warrant his withdrawal.

* * *

There has been speculation of the two riders teaming up for the 2014 Tour de France. Team Sky has more than hinted at this being a dream tour team for them. But, as the history of cycling has shown, it might just as easily present itself as a nightmare.

The Wiggins affair has shown clearly that Froome has an edge to him. After his victory in the 2012 Tour de France and then the gold in the Olympics the same year, Wiggins was a national hero. 'Wiggo' became a cultural icon – the kid from Kilburn who made good. The British public adored his eccentric ways – his sideburns, his collection of guitars and his occasional PR disasters for speaking his mind. He was the UK's first Tour de France champion. He became Sir Bradley Wiggins. He was voted the BBC Sports Personality of the Year. His face is on television ads in the UK. He wouldn't care to live in the millionaire's paradise of Monaco, as does Froome. He prefers his home in down-to-earth Lancashire, having memorably referred to Monaco as a 'shit hole'. Wiggins is exactly the kind of British bloke the average guy would want to sit down in the pub with for a pint. The Brits can empathise with Wiggins and his tough childhood with a father who was distant and not very loving. He has had his fair share of troubles in his career, many of them self-inflicted. He could be charming the one day and grumpy the next, like most people. 'Wiggo' was real to them. Towards the end of 2012, Wiggins was on top of his world. But within a few months, his entire future in road racing was in question. His position in a team he knew so well, and with the same people he had come through his career with at British Cycling, was in serious doubt. He was beginning to appear fractured and unstable in media interviews. The darling of British cycling was isolated, questioning his own existence in the sport. All because of Chris Froome. It would not be inaccurate to suggest that Froome was directly responsible for Wiggins being sidelined in such dramatic fashion.

It speaks a great deal about the edge that Froome possesses that he was able to almost single-handedly knock Wiggins of such a lofty pedestal so quickly and so ruthlessly. To the point that Team Sky have not rallied behind Wiggins in any way. It showed that although Chris Froome is a nice guy, he certainly knows how to play rough. The British public have picked up on this as well. In South Africa, Froome is very much the darling of his sport; in the UK, he is very much the silent assassin. They view him as hard, calculating and incredibly talented. This does nothing to detract from their respect for him. That is the difference – the British respect Froome, but they love Wiggins.

Froome proved himself a very good tactician in the 2013 Tour de France. But it has been the way he has negotiated his way through the politics of the peloton, most notably off the bike, that has shown Froome to be every bit as calculating as he needs to be in a very cut-throat sport.

Even his rivals are beginning to see this side of him. The man they once didn't deem worthy of riding alongside them in the peloton is now respected in the bunch. But Froome's calmness and cool demeanour during races are almost eerily reminiscent of somebody just biding his time for the ultimate attack.

On the second-last day of the 2013 Tour de France, Froome's hitherto greatest rival, Alberto Contador, was still attacking as best as he could. Contador knew he was well and truly beaten. Froome knew he had the tour sewn up and nicely packaged. It was over. There was no longer a fight. Contador even admitted as such, declaring several times how Froome was just better than him. Better than all of them. But Contador does not know how to stop fighting. He will go down swinging every single time. And even on this final day, he was still throwing punches. He may have been thoroughly beaten by Froome in the greatest race of all, but that doesn't mean he wasn't going to keep attacking and giving it to Froome for as long as he could. At one point, he and Froome were riding alongside each other. Contador softened ever so slightly. He congratulated Froome on his win. Froome was faultlessly polite, saying, 'Thank you, Alberto.' But Contador still wanted his place on the podium. He wanted to be able to walk away from this tour with something.

Then Contador asked Froome not to attack. Whether he did so as a joke or as a genuine request, only he will know. Froome had won. There was no need for another attack, another display of his awesome climbing power on the last climb of the tour. Back off a bit and savour the triumph – let me at least have this one. Froome would have lost nothing by granting it. He was so far in the lead, it would have made no difference. How did Chris Froome respond? He didn't answer Contador. Not in words, anyway. He put his head down and dropped the Spaniard on the climb. He buried him one final time, and it was just enough to see Contador finish fourth. He knocked him off the podium with one last punch to a man already staggering.

Polite, but no less powerful. Humble, but no less hard. Respectful, but no less ruthless.

Chris Froome has quietly been learning the lessons he needs to learn. In the case of Wiggins in particular, Froome showed just how costly it can be to underestimate the shy, friendly, nice guy from Africa.

Doping deliverance?

Chris Froome @chrisfroome   8 July 2012
Critics need to wake up and realise that cycling
has evolved. Dedication and sacrifice = results.
End of story!

(Froome tweeted this during the 2012 Tour de France.)

Legendary American cyclist Steve Tilford is not used to beating about the bush. This is a man who stitches up his own wounds, often by the side of the road, if he gets a gash during a race. And he's even been willing to slap his body on a vet's table for emergency surgery rather than wait his turn in hospital.

Tilford has been racing on bicycles since he was 14. He's been a professional since 1986. He has raced in Europe for several seasons. He won the first US mountain-bike championship at a time when there wasn't even a term to describe what Tilford and a handful of pioneers were doing with these off-road bikes. In 2000 he was inducted into the Mountain Bike Hall of Fame. At 53, he is still riding, racing and winning. And he still has plenty to say about a sport he has been involved in competitively since 1975.

Tilford watched almost every turn of the wheel in the 2013 Tour de France. And he wasn't convinced. During the race, he sat down at his computer to write his cycling blog:

> What seems so wrong to me about how Chris Froome is riding is that he obviously has the best power-to-weight ratio. He can climb a level above every other rider in the race by far. And he can do this at will. But he also seems to just have the most power of anyone in the race. He came within a stone's throw of winning the relatively flat individual TT [time trial – stage 11 on 10 July, where Froome finished second, only 12 seconds behind Tony Martin in the 33-kilometre time trial] a few days ago when he weighs next to nothing and has nearly as much wind resistance as other guys that have 10–15 kg [more] of body weight. This doesn't make any sense.

Elsewhere on the internet, cycling fans were asking similar questions in their blogs and forums. From the start of the 2013 Tour de France to its finish, fans, journalists and scientists were all asking the question, is this clean? It's the legacy of their betrayal by Lance Armstrong and so many others for so many years. How can we believe that what we are seeing is real?

And the same question was posed by Tilford:

> We've been shown a bunch of unreal bike racing the last couple [of] decades. We need to reset our beliefs about what should and does happen during a stage race. The same guy shouldn't always have the best day on the most important stages. There are 200 exceptional athletes in this race. A

guy should be able to ride in the *gruppetto* [the group of cyclists who have become separated by the leading group in a race], resting up, and then have a stellar day. The rider in the yellow jersey has to expend an enormous amount of energy protecting that jersey, plus an enormous amount of energy doing off-the-bike obligations. Froome seems to have more than enough energy for all of that.

The fans were not the only ones watching Froome and the rest of the peloton closely. Halfway around the world, South African sports scientist Ross Tucker sat with his laptop, a cellphone, a stopwatch, and a head full of data from watching and analysing performances in the last five Tours de France.

Tucker had watched how Froome had dominated the peloton in the stage 8 climb to Ax 3 Domaines, in the Pyrenees. Froome took the yellow jersey for the first time with one of the most dominant climbs ever seen. His time of 23 minutes and 12 seconds was faster than Lance Armstrong's on the same climb in 2003 (23:25). It was the third-fastest time in the history of the tour on this climb – faster than the performances by convicted dopers Jan Ullrich and Ivan Basso. (When he was a cyclist in high school, Froome had supported Basso, but says he immediately stopped when he found out he was doping.) It led Tucker to contemplate two possible conclusions: Chris Froome was either one exceptional individual, or ...

When I sit down with him over coffee at the Sports Science Institute of South Africa, in Cape Town, Tucker reveals just how much of a grey area cycling currently occupies as it tries to recover from the legacy of the doping era. As Tucker puts it, the entire sport is wrestling with the problem that people have 'seen this movie too often'. Cycling's history has shown us that exceptional performances are to be regarded with suspicion.

Tucker and other sports scientists, such as Antoine Vayer and Michael Puchowicz, have been applying their minds to find the most reliable system of data analysis for a cyclist's performance in the Tour de France. Each has his own system of performance analysis. And each his own motivation.

For Tucker, it is more a search for optimism that drives him and his research, rather than a witch-hunt to catch dopers. He wants to prove that cycling is clean, rather than that it is still tainted. So he does what every good scientist should do – he asks questions: 'Performance analysis is a process of asking questions. We're not just judging cyclists guilty because they're too fast. There is a rationale behind it. Cycling is all about legs and lungs, and if you know certain physiological characteristics, then you can start predicting certain outcomes. But if people are using it to say this performance is a sign of doping, then they should be run out of town.'

Essentially, the scientists – and almost everyone in cycling these days – are looking at power output, or wattage. By taking into account factors such as the length and gradient of a climb, the weight of the rider and his bike, wind resistance and basic human physiology, they use physics to calculate the watts per kilogram that the rider produces. The climbs are chosen as the best examples for these measurements because they remove variable factors such as speed, course design and wind resistance. Anything above 6 watts per kilogram is thought to deserve a second look. During his stage 8 climb up Ax 3 Domaines, Froome was calculated to have produced over 6 watts per kilogram. His time of 23:12 over a distance of 7.8 kilometres and at a gradient of 8.2 per cent was faster than that of doper Lance Armstrong, and the third-fastest performance of all time on this stage. In an article by Puchowicz in *Outside* magazine, where he was asked to dissect Froome's performance, he explained that, apart from Froome's, all the other nine fastest times up the same climb came at the height of doping during the Tour de France. Significantly, wrote Puchowicz, Richie Porte's time of 24:05 put him second behind Froome up Ax 3 Domaines, but he fell outside the top 20 on the all-time list.

The scientists immediately took to their computers. And, suddenly, the beauty, skill and romance of cycling is reduced to watts, DpVAMs and percentages, which turn it into something like science fiction.

'Let's just get straight to it,' Puchowicz wrote in his Veloclinic blog after watching Froome on his ascent of Ax 3 Domaines. 'Froome just put two DpVAM bars solidly up on Ax 3 going 4.5% faster than the 2008-2013 GT baseline and 1.9% faster than the 2002-2007 dopers.'

It sounds complicated, but in short it meant the red flags were going up everywhere. The Doper VAM (DpVAM) is a means of analysis that allows for the comparison of results across different eras and climbs in the race. Two bars up points to a suspicious performance, and two bars down indicates all is within the bounds of what can be explained in terms of normal human endurance potential. And it is that word, 'normal', that stirs up the most controversy in this debate. While he was doping, Armstrong would refer to 'not normal' as a sign that his opponents were doping or, even worse for Armstrong, had stumbled upon even better doping methods and drugs. But what is normal in cycling and what is not is still a fiercely debated topic today.

The DpVAM process begins as follows. The first step is to look at the rider's time. Then a VAM analysis is run. VAM, Italian for *velocità ascensionale media* (average climbing speed), looks at the rate of vertical ascent by a rider. Basically, it is a measure of how fast a rider is going uphill, taking into account the power output combined with the body weight of the rider. It was pioneered by Italian doctor and cycling coach Michele Ferrari, who in 2012 was handed a lifetime ban by the United States Anti-Doping Agency for drug violations. Ferrari was Armstrong's personal doctor and a man described as so brilliant and innovative as to have changed the face of cycling. Unfortunately, it was largely for the worse, as he pioneered and facilitated so much of the doping, particularly on behalf of Armstrong.

VAM measures climbing speed in terms of vertical metres per hour. But as a statistical measure, VAM has its shortcomings, failing to take into account elements such as the gradient of the climb, altitude, weather conditions, road surface and even tactics.

Scott Richards took this further when he developed pVAM – the predicted VAM of a climb taken from a historical baseline group of riders. For the purposes of the Tour de France, the pVAM was taken from the 'clean era' after the introduction of the biological passport in cycling in 2008. The biological blood passport profiles the results of a rider's doping tests over a period of time and aims to detect variances that could indicate banned substances. According to the World Anti-Doping Agency, the biological passport is designed to reveal the effects of doping rather than the doping substance itself. The blood of a cyclist, or any endurance athlete, is the epicentre in this instance. It all comes down to boosting the red blood cells in the body, which carry the oxygen. More red blood cells mean more oxygen, which means better endurance performance. The biological passport serves as a kind of DNA for each individual athlete. Multiple samples of an athlete's blood are taken over a period of time and stored for comparison. Any abnormalities are then investigated. At present, the biological passport is seen as the most effective anti-doping mechanism in sport. Armstrong even admitted that it changed his approach to doping.

The pVAM is then compared with the aVAM (actual VAM) of a climb. Later, the DpVAM was developed to add the statistics of what was achieved on climbs at the height of doping in cycling. So all of these models are various means to ask as many questions as possible without the actual available data. The cyclists and their teams are notoriously secretive about data, some even to the extent of being obstructive about providing access to this data. Hence, none of these models are an absolute science.

'Performance analysis asks questions, it does not answer them,' explains Tucker. 'It doesn't deserve outright dismissal and it doesn't warrant embracing as conclusive proof of anything.'

In other words, the calculations cannot prove a cyclist is doping, or, for that matter, disprove it.

But Froome's data revealed he was faster up Ax 3 Domaines than even the DpVAM. Yet all the other riders in the 2013 tour were slower than the DpVAM. Froome's power output – 6.37 watts per kilogram over the roughly 23-minute climb – was described by French journalist and former Festina team trainer Antoine Vayer as 'miraculous' and 'mutant' when it came to the levels of human endurance.

Tucker is far more circumspect, however, than many of the sports scientists, and believes Vayer is extreme in his assertions:

> When Chris Froome rides away from a field on the first week of the tour at a power output that is higher than bench-marked, and produces a time that puts him in the company of known dopers, we should ask questions of that performance. But we cannot conclusively use it to prove that he is doping. That would be extremism, and it would be wrong. It's for this reason that I believe Vayer is far too extreme when he declares performances 'mutant'. They are not – they're still within the realms of physiological plausibility, though on the high side.

However, Tucker is not willing to go as far as some and dismiss Vayer's findings entirely. After all, this is the man who was closer to this topic than almost anyone during his time with Festina. Team Festina was at the centre of the doping storm in the 1998 Tour de France. A Festina team car was found with a boot full of doping products. It led to a criminal court case in which nine Festina riders admitted to using EPO (erythropoietin) during the tour that year.

More shocking than this discovery and the sight of the police swarming all over a race is what was in all those little bottles, and how this substance changed cycling forever.

The message in the bottle

'With EPO ... you can recover, rebalance, and keep going at the same level.'

Erythropoietin has become the scourge of professional cycling. But, for the riders who used it illegally, it was heaven in a bottle.

EPO occurs naturally in the body as a hormone. Its job is to stimulate the bone marrow to produce red blood cells, which carry the oxygen through the body. As a commercial product, it was developed to help patients on dialysis and with cancer to combat anaemia. But it wasn't long before its benefits were discovered by endurance athletes. Studies have shown that EPO can boost an endurance athlete's performance by 10–15 per cent – a giant leap in a sport such as cycling, where 5 per cent in the Tour de France can mean the difference between victory and finishing in the bunch.

Tyler Hamilton, who raced in the same US Postal team as Lance Armstrong at the height of the doping era in the Tour de France, and who was eventually found guilty of doping and became the sport's most significant whistle-blower, said that 'EPO changed everything. Amphetamines and anabolics are nothing compared to EPO.'

For a long time, Hamilton resisted the temptation to dope. But he paints a brilliant portrait of the challenge of racing against doped riders, giving an insight into why cyclists at the time were saying you couldn't win the Tour de France without doping.

'All of a sudden whole teams were ragingly fast ... By 1994, it was ridiculous. I'd be on climbs, working as hard as I'd ever worked, producing exactly the same power, at the same weight, and right alongside me would be these big-assed guys, and they'd be chatting like we were on the flats! It was completely crazy,' Hamilton says in his co-authored groundbreaking book *The Secret Race – Inside the Hidden World of the Tour de France*.

But surely you could just train harder than the riders on EPO, and that would allow you to beat them? As Hamilton explains, it depended on the race:

For shorter races, even week-long stage races, I think the answer is a qualified yes ... But once you get past a one-week race, it quickly becomes impossible for clean riders to compete with riders using Edgar [their code name for EPO, as in Edgar Allan Poe], because Edgar is too big of an advantage. The longer the race, the bigger the advantage becomes – hence the power of Edgar in the Tour de France. The reason is cost, in the physiological sense. Big efforts – winning Alpine stages, winning time trials – cost too much energy; they cause the body to break down ... Without Edgar ... those costs add up. With Edgar ... you can recover, rebalance, and keep going at the same level.

Contrary to popular belief, EPO is not necessarily for the lazy cyclist. It is not the substitute for training. Rather, it is the ultimate enhancer. When an endurance athlete hits the wall at the limits of his performance, EPO is the hammer that allows him to break through. Hamilton writes:

> Suddenly there's a feeling of new possibility. Fear melts. You wonder: How far could I go? How fast can I ride? … EPO granted the ability to suffer more; to push yourself farther and harder than you'd ever imagined, in both training and racing.
>
> It feels great, mostly because it doesn't feel like anything at all. You're not wiped out. You feel healthy, normal, strong … These little clear drops work like radio signals – they instruct your bone marrow to create more red blood cells, and soon millions more are filling up your veins, carrying oxygen to your muscles. Everything else about your body is the same, except now you have better fuel. You can go harder, longer. That holy place at the edge of your limits gets nudged out – and not just a little.

As Vayer was there when EPO was blown out into the open, Tucker argues that he knows a lot more than most, which immediately makes him credible. 'Everyone is like, "Oh this nut job, this pseudo scientist." He was the first guy in the world to know what's going on because he was right there with Festina. That's why it's so foolish for people to say, "What does Vayer know?" Vayer knows more than anyone.'

But there are also flaws in Vayer's analysis and inter-pretations of Froome's performance. The calculations do not take into account the fact that Ax 3 Domaines was the first major climb of the tour, coming in the first week, when the riders are all still relatively fresh. It is also one of the shortest. Generally, the data concluded that the performances on Ax 3 Domaines were within what could be considered a relatively clean peloton. Except for Froome – who produced numbers outside of these bounds and entered a realm considered at the very limits of clean human potential.

Dr Fred Grappe, the physiologist for *L'Équipe* and the French Cycling Federation's scientific adviser for several years, was reportedly given access to Froome's data for the previous two years, data that included 18 climbs, by Team Sky manager, David Brailsford, after repeated pressure and questioning by the media following another explosive climb by Froome up Mont Ventoux later in the race.

Grappe applied his own method of analysis, the record power profile (RPP), which is the maximum power a rider can sustain over a set period. 'Froome's RPP over two years shows no fundamental anomaly. In two years, his profile has not changed,' Grappe wrote in *L'Équipe*.

In a sense, Grappe's analysis vindicated what Froome and Brailsford had been saying during the tour, and perhaps showed that Team Sky's reluctance to release all of its data was based more on fear of giving its competitors an advantage rather than having something to hide. After all, this is a team that speaks of 'marginal gains' and has made a science of the smallest details necessary for success in cycling.

But many observers aren't buying all of it. There was a sense among sceptics that there was a very orchestrated public-relations campaign by Team Sky during the 2013 Tour de France. Stories were being released to the media about how Froome had produced this amazing result in training before the tour, and how he represented the 'new normal'. During the tour, stories emerged about Froome's diet, then his amazing VO_2 (capacity to transport and use oxygen), and his physiology. Questions were also asked about what exactly the data was that Grappe analysed, and whether it represented anything significant at all to warrant Grappe's conclusion that Froome's performance was plausible.

At the other end of the spectrum, Brailsford was becoming increasingly frustrated at having to answer questions about doping that he felt he could not. The challenge lies in proving a negative. Brailsford told journalists after the Ventoux ascent:

I'm trying to defend someone who has done nothing wrong. I'm happy to do it and more than happy to try and convince you guys that we're not doing anything wrong but we need a bit of help. Why don't you collectively have a meeting, get yourself together, get organised, and you tell me what could we do so we wouldn't have to answer these questions. Because you're asking me to come up with some sort of novel idea to satisfy you ... I know what we're doing but I haven't got a magic wand to help come and convince you guys, so help me out.

You're asking me how can I prove to you that we're not doping, basically ... Every day we get asked the same question and I can assure you we think really hard about the optimal way to prove to you guys that we're not doping.

The simple-enough solution would be to release all of the data for every rider during all the major races. But this is where cycling is a closed book. 'When you watch an 800-metre race, it's compelling because you get the 200-metre splits and you can estimate performance and so on. But cycling gives us nothing,' says Tucker. 'At the end of a stage we're told he did it in 5 hours and 13 minutes. Great. But what does that actually tell us? Just make the data available to us.'

Yet teams remain unwilling to do this. The argument is that this is a team's competitive advantage – although Brailsford has suggested they would be willing to provide this information to identified experts at the World Anti-Doping Agency. Tucker is quite happy to draw the line when it comes to data.

'Some people are arguing that Sky should release their training data. Well, I wouldn't even consider it. Then you're giving away your training information and that would be foolish. But, your race data, why not? At the moment, we're all estimating using three or four different models, and those are fairly good, but not perfect. If we had data, then the whole debate could be taken to the next level. You can start to answer all the questions we have.'

But Tucker does not subscribe to the argument that Sky are doing something revolutionary in their training that they want to conceal from other teams:

I've done a bit of work with UK Olympic sport. Cycling is probably their flagship sport in terms of how well it's done and what they're trying to do in all of their sports. It's unbelievable how good they are. They are so meticulous and methodical. Everything is analysed, from the management and organisational structures to the talent identification and the funding. They've got the best people, they don't spare any expense.

But I don't believe that Sky are doing new things. For example, they said they do little things like putting pineapple juice in the water to make it taste better so the riders drink more. Give me a break – that was being done 30 years ago. Sky also say they brought in Tim Kerrison from swimming and he's brought new ideas to the team. Swimming is way behind cycling in terms of coaching and training. So, for me, it's unlikely that they're bringing new things in.

They also say their technology is better, their sports science is better. I find it implausible and a little disrespectful to the other teams because cycling has the best sports scientists.

What I do think is that, because of their budget and attention to detail, they might do the same things better than everyone else. But I don't think they're doing better things.

In his exasperation to convince sceptics that his riders are clean, Brailsford has become increasingly impatient with what he terms cycling's 'pseudo science', the so-called armchair scientists investigating and questioning the likes of Froome. For a man with an acute sense of tactics, this has been one of Brailsford's mistakes.

'Labelling people who are trying to analyse this as "pseudo scientists", as David Brailsford did, well that fuelled their desire to do it. There were a good few guys who went on the attack because of that comment,' says Tucker.

And the question most return to all of the time is, what is the limit of human endurance? Despite his validation of Froome's data, Grappe concluded that Froome's performances on Ax 3 Domaines and Ventoux were at the current known limit of human physiology. Scientists are trying to establish plausible physiology and plausible performance. In other words, there are certain physiological laws to which all clean athletes have to adhere. And these, in turn, produce certain physiological results. As Tucker explains, the best way to understand this is to take the example of a car. If you were holding a speed camera and a car came past you at 350 km/h, you would rightly assume that this car had a 6-litre engine in it, or your camera was faulty. It couldn't be a 1.3-litre Tazz because it just wouldn't make sense. It is exactly the same concept when it comes to cycling: if a cyclist is able to produce a given performance in terms of power output, then he has to have certain physiological parameters. Otherwise, as American cyclist Greg LeMond pointed out with Alberto Contador after his incredible ride up Verbier in the 2009 Tour de France, the physiological implications are just unrealistic. So there must be something else involved.

However, when it comes to establishing these physiological parameters, you have to make certain assumptions. And this is where cycling once again enters that big grey area. Tucker explains:

You have to assume best case, worst case. You have to play with both extremes. In the case of cycling, to give the benefit of the doubt to the cyclist, you have to always assume the best-case scenario. So let's assume this rider has amazing efficiency [the oxygen cost of a cyclist to generate a given power output], let's assume he has amazing VO_2 max [maximum capacity to transport and use oxygen], let's assume he has an amazing sustained lactate threshold [the point in exercise at which lactic acid starts to accumulate in the blood stream and slows the muscles – the delay of this in an athlete is key to a higher level of performance], then what could he do?

There are certain rules of nature here. In a particular cyclist, the VO_2 max and efficiency are never both high: one is always high and the other is low. Again, it's like a car. A fuel-efficient car will never have a big engine, and vice versa. So, when estimating the best clean performance of a rider, the physiologists would assume that his VO_2 max is high, his sustained lactate threshold is high, but he has low efficiency. From this, they would work out the predicted performance of this individual.

When you do high, high, high for all of these, the power output you get to is about 6.5 watts per kilogram for 45 minutes. So you would effectively be saying that this particular cyclist can ride Alpe d'Huez at 6.4 or 6.5 watts a kilogram and he will do it in 37 minutes, 20 seconds. That's the simple model, the best-case scenario. If you had to design a human being in a laboratory, that's what you would do. However, as Tucker explains,

the realistic-case scenario is that he's slightly lower on the efficiency, so now we're looking at 38 minutes on Alpe d'Huez. And when you play with those numbers, you discover that there's a sort of grey area, call it a plausibility zone or an orange zone, of between 5.9 and 6.3 or 6.4 watts a kilogram. Anything above that, and then you really have to start scraping the barrel for assumptions. You have to start saying, 'Okay, maybe this rider has a kind of never-seen-before efficiency, maybe he just has unbelievable lactate threshold numbers.' But it gets to the point where it just doesn't add up, where you have to make too many ridiculous assumptions. And I've been doing this for the last five Tours de France, and what we're seeing is that pretty much all of the winners of these Tours are in this orange zone.

Did they get there because of doping? 'Well, you can't say yes or no either way. Are they there naturally? Well, they could be. You're never going to definitively answer that question until it becomes so ridiculously obvious.'

The dominance of the US Postal team under Armstrong in the Tour de France was a perfect example of reaching these ridiculous levels. It just wasn't possible that an entire team of riders could, day in and day out, be riding at the front of the peloton and destroying everybody else without the slightest sign of fatigue. It became so obvious that something was up. But what happens when it's not that obvious? What happens when it's just in this area of uncertainty, where you can't dismiss it outright, but you also have nagging questions. That's the position where a cyclist such as Froome finds himself. And Tucker is happy to go on asking those questions, but without being too quick to accuse:

We shouldn't be accusing, just wondering. And given cycling's history, and the fact that those entrusted with running the sport have shown themselves to be unable to clean it up, we cannot simply believe blindly in miracles this time around. So we wonder, reasonably, and use some kind of performance metric to gain some insight. Proof, no. But, equally, not worthless.

In cycling, people seem to have either blindly embraced or discarded the concept of performance analysis, whether it be for the metric time up a mountain, estimated power output or the physiological implications of that performance, without recognising the necessary nuance.

Performance analysis in cycling does not replace common sense or give permission to disengage every other sense in order to rigidly accept a black-and-white version of the world of sport, which is clearly nuanced and everyone recognises this. For this reason, it never constitutes proof.

Tucker does not buy into any form of extremism when it comes to performance analysis and the numbers it represents. Instead, he would like it to be seen as one element in helping solve the greater riddle. Much in the same way that a human needs to employ all five senses, he believes relying solely on performance analysis as proof of doping is a mistake.

So Tucker argues against reading Froome's Ax 3 Domaines ascent data in isolation from the rest of the tour, and to be more circumspect.

'I use the term "performance pixilation". If you look only at Chris Froome's Ax 3 Domaines and Mont Ventoux performances, he looks guilty as hell because he's faster than the dopers were.'

For the scientists, Ax 3 Domaines and Mont Ventoux are not the best barometers of performance in the Tour de France because they have not featured as regularly throughout the history of the race. Tucker explains:

If you look at his performance on Alpe d'Huez, which has featured 27 times in the tour, he's 86th or something in the tour's history. So you can't just look at one climb and get stuck on that, which people tend to do. I would like to look at Chris Froome over the next three or four years. But, more importantly, I'd also like to look at the top 50 riders in the tour and what they're doing. With performance analysis we are really only scratching the surface. We're only analysing the top three or four riders, and we don't have a frame of reference because we didn't do it in the same detail 15 years ago when doping was obviously a big problem, or even ten years ago when it was still a problem. So what are we comparing it to?

The pVAM method is just a case of gathering as much historical data as possible. So, if this is typical in the past, where are we in relation to this? The key assumption to that method is that the past is a valid comparison to the present. If this is my benchmark, then I need to be sure this set of data represents a clean set of performances. It's a good concept. The problem, though, is that I don't think there's enough data for that method, so that means one rider who is a slight outlier can look like a doper. What we should've been doing is analysing what's the average of the top ten or 20, and even 50, riders.

Analysing the performance of the best rider in the Tour de France is the most obvious point of departure. But, at the front of the race, there are so many other factors that influence what's happening, such as tactics, the state of the race and the environment. Statistics on the top 50 riders offer a much bigger data set for a scientist to draw from and, consequently, would give more meaning to the numbers. If there was less doping, you would see that in the times of the top 50 riders. The best might stay the same, but everyone else would get slower.

This variability is key to the doping debate – variability of a cyclist's performance in an extended stage race. In the Armstrong era, there was no variability. The riders were all at their best every single day because the drugs made that possible. The attacks were also coming from further out – long-distance attacks that were just not possible.

In a clean race, there is a cost. Doping means you don't have to pay the cost. Doping removes the interest payments. Without doping you pay the interest – big effort today, and tomorrow you might pay for it.

* * *

Froome's stance, though, is that there was never a debate or a doubt about doping or his performances in the 2013 Tour de France. 'Lance cheated. I'm not cheating. End of story,' he told journalists after the Ventoux climb. Unfortunately for Froome, however, the first winner of the Tour de France following Armstrong's doping revelations, it is far from the end of the story. But it was the first time Froome showed visible signs of cracking under the pressure of constant questions around doping.

Throughout the tour, Froome explained how he saw himself as the man ready to right the doping wrongs in cycling and prove that exceptional performances could be clean performances.

His greatest rival, Alberto Contador, who served a two-year ban for testing positive for clenbuterol, a drug that can enhance an athlete's aerobic capacity and ability to metabolise fat, during the 2010 Tour de France, was quick to leap to Froome's defence. 'There is no reason to doubt about Froome,' the Spaniard told reporters after Ventoux. 'He is a professional rider who has been performing at a really high level all year, and I think that his results are the fruits of the work he puts in and nothing else. I fully believe that he is clean. That is why the doping controls are there, isn't it?'

Froome clearly knew he was going to face a barrage of doping questions in the 2013 Tour de France, as perhaps any rider post-Armstrong would – even more so as the wearer of the yellow jersey. And Team Sky had obviously prepared for it, confident that the usually calm and reserved Froome would handle the questions better than their 2012 winner, Bradley Wiggins.

During the 2012 Tour, Wiggins launched into several tirades against journalists and fans whenever questioned about doping. 'I say they're just fucking wankers. I cannot be doing with people like that. It justifies their own bone idleness because they can't ever imagine applying themselves to doing anything in their lives. It's easy for them to sit under a pseudonym on Twitter and write that sort of shit rather than get off their arses in their own lives and apply themselves and work hard at something and achieve something.'

This outburst was a strange role reversal for the man who, early in his career, was one of the most outspoken when it came to dopers in cycling, and called for their expulsion from the sport.

In 2007 Wiggins was in the Cofidis team, which withdrew from the tour when his Italian teammate Cristian Moreni tested positive for testosterone doping after the 11th stage.

'I don't want to continue in the Tour anyway. It is not supposed to be like this,' Wiggins told the *Guardian* at the time. 'Everyone knows where I stand on doping. I have nothing to hide.'

When, during the 2012 Tour de France, Wiggins was cross-examined about doping, one of his outlets was to resort to a statement in the *Guardian* in which he had declared:

The question that needs to be asked is not why wouldn't I take drugs, but why would I? I know exactly why I wouldn't dope. To start with, I come to professional road-racing from a different background to a lot of guys. There is a different culture in British cycling. Britain is a country where doping is not morally acceptable. I was born in Belgium but I grew up in the British environment, with the Olympic side of the sport as well as the Tour de France. I don't care what people say, the attitude to doping in the UK is different to in Italy or France maybe, where a rider like Richard Virenque can dope, be caught, be banned, come back and be a national hero.

If I doped I would potentially stand to lose everything. It's a long list. My reputation, my livelihood, my marriage, my family, my house. Everything I have achieved, my Olympic medals, my world titles, the CBE I was given. I would have to take my children to the school gates in a small Lancashire village with everyone looking at me, knowing I had cheated, knowing I had, perhaps, won the Tour de France, but then been caught. I remember in 2007 throwing that Cofidis kit in the bin at that small airport, where no one knew me, because I didn't want any chance of being associated with doping. Then I imagine how it would be in a tiny community where everyone knows everyone.

But now Wiggins was saying he was not the moral keeper of the Tour de France. Clearly, the stated intention of Sky to win the tour clean in the wake of the Lance Armstrong era was weighing heavily on him, and Wiggins said he was done with being labelled 'the whistle-blower' as he was dubbed on the cover of a cycling magazine in 2006. During the doping era, there was said to be the cyclist's code of *omertà*, a mafia-style moral obligation to keep the secrets of the peloton. Break it, and you were cast as an outsider.

Wiggins, and Froome in 2013, have both felt somewhat victimised in the fallout caused by Armstrong, in the sense that he has left them to answer all the tough questions. 'We are the ones here, in this sport, right now, who have to pick up the pieces ... the ones sitting there in front of the press trying to convince them of our innocence, continuing to do things in the right way; they've trashed the office and left; we're the ones trying to tidy it all up,' said Wiggins.

Yet, even such a public confession is still not enough: the

legacy of the Armstrong saga is that an uneasy relationship now exists not only between the cyclists and the media, but between the cyclists and their fans as well. The cyclists feel they deserve greater trust in this new era, but the fans feel they haven't yet earned it.

The result is the kind of righteous indignation displayed by Wiggins and, to a far milder extent, by Froome. How can you not believe that my sheer hard work produces these results? What more proof can I give you? And the fans and journalists are becoming tired of being labelled as fat, useless underachievers purely because they are asking questions about the legitimacy of performances. Says Tucker:

Chris Froome had that press conference where he made that unfortunate statement about how the team spent weeks near a volcano working their arses off. Well, those kinds of arguments are now inadmissible in cycling because Lance Armstrong took them away from you. And the more defensive Froome and his camp get, the more they look like Lance. So just let it go.

If I could speak to Chris Froome, I would say the first point is you have no right to be angry with the fans and the media. If you want to be angry with someone, then it's Lance Armstrong. Not for doping, because the truth is that most riders in that same situation would have doped. But the problem is that Lance was so aggressive about it and he was so nasty and mafia-like. That's taken away Froome's credibility. It wasn't so much that Lance doped, it was the way that he did it.

I've yet to hear Chris Froome say, 'I'm just so pissed off

at Lance because he undermined all our hard work with his campaign in the media.' I spoke to Tyler Hamilton and he was saying that at the time it was happening he couldn't criticise other dopers. Even now he doesn't want to do so because he knows how hard it is, and he's guilty and doesn't want to appear hypocritical. So as a cyclist, there are two reasons you wouldn't criticise a doper. One is you're a doper yourself and you can't do it without making yourself a hypocrite. And the other is you're surrounded by these people all the time and why would you want to create animosity by being nasty about someone else? I'm still amazed that no cyclist has really come out against Lance for his bullying, his lies, his nastiness, and the fact that he was so actively against the media.

The other day, I read that Froome was saying for blood doping there should be instant life bans. That's fair because sometimes you can get a testosterone positive test accidentally or a stimulant accidentally. But you're not going to get someone else's blood in your body by mistake. The same for EPO. That doesn't happen by accident. So when Froome speaks like that, then it gives me confidence. Now he's making the right noises.

But cyclists' defence of each other within their own ranks is also becoming more aggressive. Armstrong wielded a power rarely seen by an athlete, largely because of the army of supporters around him.

Although Froome is described as a mild-mannered, humble man, his fiancée and PR manager, Michelle Cound, can be combative at times, as displayed in her running Twit-

Chris Froome had to ride in the shadow of Bradley Wiggins in the 2012 Tour de France, but had started showing signs of being a future grand tour contender.
AAI/FOTOSTOCK

As the first winner of the Tour de France following Lance Armstrong's public confession of doping, Froome was always going to be in the spotlight.
GREATSTOCK/CORBIS

CONTRÔLE
ANTI-DOPAGE

Lance Armstrong was famous for what became known as 'the look'. In the 2012 Tour de France, Froome's glance back at Wiggins after he unexpectedly accelerated past him during stage 11 caused controversy and heightened rumours of a rift between the two riders. GALLO IMAGES/AFP

Chris Froome is satisfied that he has ushered in a new era of clean cycling in the Tour de France. GALLO IMAGES/AFP

As his fiancée and public-relations manager, Michelle Cound is Froome's most loyal supporter, and a fierce defender of his claim of being a clean cyclist. GALLO IMAGES/AFP

The Tour de France remains one of the most gruelling physical challenges in sport. BRYN LENNON/GETTY IMAGES/GALLO IMAGES

What the young Chris Froome could only have dreamt of – cycling beneath the Arc de Triomphe as winner of the Tour de France. THE BIGGERPICTURE/REUTERS

As he stood on the podium, Chris Froome declared to the world that his Tour de France victory would stand the test of time. THE BIGGERPICTURE/REUTERS

ter battles with Catherine Wiggins over everything from Froome's questionable loyalty to Wiggins in the 2012 tour, to the Wigginses' alleged failure to congratulate Froome on winning the 2013 Tour. Tucker has also fallen foul of Cound:

> I had a long Facebook argument with her. She doesn't seem to understand the sport. She doesn't seem to have an appreciation of her own place in cycling, and Chris's place in cycling. I tried to tell her that all these arguments she is using are just making Chris look worse. You should rather be coming out against Lance because that will win you more friends. I can understand it must be hard when you win a stage and the first question is, 'Chris, how did you do that without doping?' But an aggressive defence around Froome makes people sceptical and hostile.
>
> And you can't make the argument she makes, namely, 'Do you think if Chris was doping I'd be so supportive of him?' Oh c'mon! Chris is a nice guy. Well, he seems like a really nice guy. I want to believe him, but it's not an argument to make for his innocence.
>
> They said the same about Tyler Hamilton and Lance Armstrong. Armstrong was said to be this saviour who would never have risked doping because of the damage it would have done to cancer survivors. Jan Ullrich was a really genuine and hard-working guy. Floyd Landis was religious and he wouldn't have doped. That's the frustration of all of this. Everyone says Chris would never risk Sky's reputation. I mean, Lance Armstrong gambled with cancer. Froome's reputation is not even nearly as valuable as Armstrong's was in that sense. The point is that someone's personality and

their doping behaviour are not related. History has shown us this many times.

Author Daniel Coyle, who wrote *The Secret Race* with Hamilton, paints a picture of Hamilton that is very similar to the image of Froome – soft-spoken, polite, tough beyond conventional measure: 'A blue-collar racer who slowly, patiently ascended the pyramid of the cycling world. Along the way, he became known for his unparalleled work ethic, his low-key, friendly personality, and, most of all, his remarkable ability to endure pain ... Hamilton was also one of the better-liked riders in the peloton: humble, quick to praise others, and considerate ... Most of the time, Hamilton was exactly as advertised: humble, nice, polite, every inch the Boy Scout.'

In short, in the wrong environment, with the right kind of pressure, even nice guys end up doping.

For those who are sceptical about Froome's performance, there's also the added similarity of another rider with a health condition – Armstrong with cancer, Froome with bilharzia. Says Tucker:

The big confounder with Froome is that he had this parasitic disease. To produce what he's doing now, physiologically, he must have extraordinary efficiency, amazing VO_2 max, or amazing lactate threshold. Those things are trainable, but only to a point. There's not much evidence that you can move those beyond a few percentage points higher. Some people are what you would call a responder and they show massive improvements. Some people can train for years and get very little. So you could assume, best case, that Froome is a really big responder. But still, when the guy is a junior and he's got that much maximum potential, even if he's a big responder you'd still say, 'Hey, this guy is quite something.' Then again, he did get a professional contract as a young rider. So someone saw something in him. So he couldn't have been below average. He was still in the top 500 in the world to get a professional contract. So define average. He was offered a contract at Sky not because he was below average.

The bilharzia sounds like a plausible explanation, but the prosecution would argue that it's just another excuse. And both have a case. That's how difficult this is. You can argue the same information in two different ways.

Froome's father, Clive, revealed his confusion about the media sceptics of his son's performances in the Tour de France. He told Sky News:

I can remember sending him an SMS after the press conference after his victory on Mont Ventoux the next morning, saying I really couldn't believe the extent to which, rather than congratulate him, the media there were pointing fingers and bringing up the issue again.

He's been passionately opposed to the use of drugs ever since he was an adolescent. I think he really feels this year it could be a landmark for cycling. He's felt pretty indignant about the aspersions cast in his direction and I think he feels that with so many young, clean riders achieving positions in this year's tour that it may be a turning point for cycling, which cycling so badly needs. And I think the cycling community will probably support him in that and continue to drive out those malevolent individuals who quietly on the side possibly still use drugs.

Froome's public disapproval of doping was at no time more strongly emphasised than in July 2008, when he rode in his first Tour de France for Team Barloworld.

On that occasion, Froome's teammate Moisés Dueñas Nevado was expelled from the race after he tested positive for EPO. Barloworld strongly denied they had anything to do with the drugs and said Dueñas had taken them in secret.

Froome was damning in his own judgement of the incident. 'The guy is facing a jail sentence and I hope that's what he gets. To have something like that so close to home was unbelievable – I never saw it coming. You just feel that you've been cheated by one of your teammates.'

Froome went further in an interview with *Cyclingnews* writer Daniel Benson that year. 'To me it's just so shocking. You always hear about doping scandals and see them in other teams. When that happens you're tempted to just turn away. But to have it happen in our team was such a shock. Moisés is a really decent guy, it's something I didn't expect from him. I've not spoken to him since and I don't think anyone on the team has, either.'

And he again showed his own zero tolerance of doping when he added, 'I'm sure he's in enough trouble as it is and that he'll regret it for the rest of his life. There's already the possibility of a two-year suspension, a jail sentence and a huge fine to pay, and I hope he accepts that. I'm sure that he'll regret it for the rest of his life. If that's the only way it's going to stop guys doping then we should throw them in jail.'

As mentioned, as a schoolboy cyclist in South Africa, Froome's first cycling hero was Italian Ivan Basso. Froome loved his status as the underdog. But when Basso was banned for doping in 2006, Froome immediately stopped supporting him.

When you're dealing with a sport where the leading race has over the past 20 years seen 75 per cent of the riders who have stood on the final podium being implicated in doping, the questions will remain.

Especially when a rider claims the biggest winning margin in the tour – 4 minutes and 20 seconds – since Armstrong won the 2004 tour by over 6 minutes.

The questions grew when Bike Pure, a group set up in 2008, which 'aims to protect the integrity of cycling and promote clean cyclesport', removed Froome from its list of endorsed riders shortly before the start of the 2013 Tour de France.

The organisation claims to have over 170 cyclists and teams aligned with it, and is said to be 'the world's largest independent anti-doping and ethical sporting organisation of its kind'. Bike Pure issued a statement on its website, parts of which read:

We contacted Team Sky's Chris Froome on this issue some weeks ago, asking if he would be willing to produce his data during or after the Tour. We didn't receive a direct response, however he did pass the email to his team. We received a phone call on 20th June from Fran Millar, Head of Business operations for Team Sky, who said Froome wouldn't be making any of his data public. Bike Pure also asked if Froome would be willing to make data available after the Tour and we have not received a response as yet.

Many will know that Froome aligned with our organisation some years ago whilst riding for Team Barloworld. We have asked for clarification from Chris on a number of occasions in the last 18 months via email and direct message on Twitter if he still wished to form part of our organisation. As a result of not receiving such clarification from Chris or Team Sky in recent days we have made the difficult decision to remove his bio page from our website. This in no way insinuates that Froome is a suspicious rider but we feel that if riders do not support our organisation then there is no reason for us to promote them as such.

Andy Layhe

Co-Founder – Bike Pure

In an update about this, Bike Pure wrote:

We have been accused ... of releasing the above statement simply for PR purposes and that Chris was singled out to release data. Therefore we would like to make some points and clarification on the issue ...

As Chris was our highest-profile rider, grand tour podium finisher and potential Tour de France winner we felt it necessary to contact him to gain written clarification of his alignment to our organisation. We initially did this in December 2012 ... We received no response.

We made several attempts to contact him ... asking to

confirm what we had asked in December 2012 ... We had no response. Shortly after, Chris chose to unfollow us on Twitter.

We felt the correct course of action was to contact his team regarding the issue and completed the contact form on the Team Sky website on two occasions asking for someone to contact us regards the issue. We received an automated reply saying our messages had been received, but we received no direct response from anyone within Team Sky until the call from Fran Millar on Thursday 20th June.

We had waited 6 months for clarification and preferred the matter was resolved before the 2013 Tour de France, therefore we set a deadline of Friday 21st June for clarification. We received a call from Fran Millar at Team Sky on Thursday 20th June stating that we had threatened Chris and that Sky would not be releasing any data simply because other teams refuse to do so either. We simply asked for clarification on Chris's alignment to Bike Pure and stated that a simple statement would resolve the issue. We received none either on the phone or in written email, therefore were left with the difficult decision to remove his bio from our website.

Again, convicted doper and now ardent anti-doping campaigner David Millar points out that there could be a very valid reason for not making Froome's data widely available: 'Sky are impressive ... I think it's impressive and we need to start copying them in a certain way,' he told Scotland's *Daily Record*. 'If we had their numbers, we would have a benchmark to aim for. We would be copying their training files, we'd have the targets and we'd know what we have to do to beat them. They don't want the other teams to know what they have to do to beat them ... If you have a recipe for training which obviously works, why would you give away that recipe?'

Millar was one of those who came to Froome's defence, saying he believed Froome was clean. But Millar had also previously told a CNN journalist that 'the moment we say it's 100% clean is the moment we're lying'.

Millar revealed how, early in his career, he had been vehemently opposed to doping. 'I was a fervent anti-doper. I was a naive kid who came from Hong Kong, who dreamed of winning the Tour de France and who was disgusted to learn that my colleagues were doping, but within four or five years I was one of them.'

And he gave insight into how quickly this can happen as he moved from vitamin injections to dope. 'I was part of a culture where ... it was never obligatory, but ... I would describe it as white noise. It was always there. It was in the background. It was something with a certain inevitability about it – if I ever wanted to be the best and be professional.'

Fuelling the questions around Sky was the controversial fact that Brailsford admitted they used the services of Belgian doctor Geert Leinders, who is under investigation for his involvement in doping during his time as the Rabobank team doctor before the 2012 Tour de France campaign.

Brailsford said at the time he was unaware of anything untoward in the team, and Leinders was not part of the staff of Team Sky during the 2012 Tour de France. 'The whole thing is my responsibility. I will take that squarely on the chin. It's something I regret. It's a mistake. I should not have done it. I made an error of judgment,' Brailsford said.

These and other inconsistencies have polarised the media and, most notably, two of cycling journalism's biggest anti-doping campaigners.

David Walsh and Paul Kimmage were the leading campaigners in the journalistic battle to prove that Armstrong was doping. In a sense, they were Watergate's Bob Woodward and Carl Bernstein in the Armstrong saga.

But the last two Tours de France and the rise of Team Sky have strained their relationship.

After the 2013 tour, Walsh wrote an article in the *Sunday Times* under the headline, 'Why I believe in Chris Froome'.

Walsh felt he could write such an article because he was part of Team Sky, and observed the Tour de France from inside the team.

In his article, he said of Froome's critics, '... it was a reminder of how Lance Armstrong was regarded. Once he was the most loved sportsman on the planet. Partly because of that betrayal, the mob was baying for Froome's blood on the Alpe. They were wrong when Armstrong was winning. They are wrong about Froome. History will correct this, as it did the Armstrong story.'

Kimmage immediately took exception. In an interview broadcast on *The Irish Times*'s podcast Second Captains, Kimmage said:

> ... two years ago Chris Froome was disqualified from the Tour
> of Italy for hanging on a motorbike going up one of the climbs.
> This year he is the standout winner of the Tour de France. To

what do we attribute this remarkable transformation? This is the problem – the transformation from a rider who was a good professional, but I don't think anybody in the sport would've looked at Froome in '08, '09 or '10 and described him as a potential Tour de France winner.

In the summer of 2011, Froome's contract was running out. By the time they got to the Vuelta in September, Team Sky still weren't sure they were going to renew it. He went to the Vuelta that year and produced an absolutely outstanding performance. So there was this radical transformation in 2011.

There are some really startling inconsistencies in what Froome and the team have said about when he got bilharzia, how he was treated, what the disease actually entails ... Everything may be as it seems. But at a time when we have somebody who beats cancer and goes on to win 7 Tours, we have someone who comes back from bilharzia and wins the Tour de France in a manner we haven't seen for a long time ... I mean, what he did on Mont Ventoux was absolutely staggering. He absolutely smoked Contador without getting out of the saddle. Now I've never seen anybody accelerate in the way that Froome did without actually lifting his arse from the saddle. It was like opening up a throttle ... To be fair, there were clear signs during this Tour that things are changing. I don't say things have changed. I say things are changing.

A similar scepticism is expressed by Steve Tilford. Responding to my email about his blog and the concerns he raised about Froome, Tilford wrote:

I've never met Chris Froome, I don't think. I've been racing bicycles since I was a child. I've ridden with the best cyclists in the world the last four decades. The change that occurred back in the early 90s was very apparent from an insider's view. There are limits to what humans can do. We aren't close to them, but the monumental leaps that occurred in the sport of cycling were make-believe. The problem is that the fans have been watching make-believe cycling for so long that they expect it to be real.

Here's the deal. I have no idea what Bradley Wiggins and Chris Froome are doing. It all might be within the rules of the sport. But they are both doing something strange to have these results. Eating something that naturally raises their oxygen-carrying capacity? I don't know. But you can't take guys that were mediocre on the road previously and make them into the best climbing and the best time-trialling riders in the world so quickly. The weight loss is very strange. The 68-kilogram rider should never beat the 80-kilogram rider in a time trial. First and third in the Olympic time trial after just finishing the Tour de France? Unheard of. Like I wrote on my website, it would be the same as the lightweight crew having faster times than the heavyweight crew in rowing. The best time at flat time trialling should not be the best climber. It has only occurred since the introduction of doping into the sport.

Another worrisome issue is the consistency of these guys. Bradley last year and Chris this year nearly never lost a race. Cycling is such a dynamic sport, randomness should occur, plus the season is so long and different that the same guy shouldn't be winning so consistently month after month during a year. That isn't how the human body behaves. I've never seen this before in modern cycling.

ESPN magazine columnist Jeff MacGregor took a more philosophical view in his column 'The Age of Innocence', where he highlighted another danger of the Armstrong legacy – the assumption of guilt:

> Sports are just a theater of the human, after all, and from the beginning of time athletes have lied and cheated. A rush to judgment is easy. But a free society rests on the principles of due process and the presumption of innocence. The cheater, the liar, the crook who gets away with it are part of the cost of democracy. 'It is better that 10 guilty persons escape than that one innocent suffer,' wrote Blackstone in his *Commentaries*.
>
> The benefit of the doubt is the price of our freedom ...
>
> We rush to build even more determined strategies and elaborate mechanisms for detection and security. Biological passports; around-the-clock surveillance; polygraph tests; watch lists. More draconian penalties ...
>
> Sure, it's just a game. But the danger lies in eventually assuming everyone everywhere is guilty of something. That everyone needs to be watched. Observed. Tested. Overseen. Overheard. Suspected. That everyone's a threat. *That's* the temptation. *That's* the real price of our cynicism and fear.
>
> The seeds of the police state lie in the presumption of guilt. In order for democracy to survive, every citizen must be granted the presumption of innocence. No matter how often we're hurt by it or made to look foolish by men like

Ryan Braun. Your freedom and mine depend upon our absolute willingness to be cheated, to be gulled, to be played for suckers again.

Some of the Italian newspapers, however, were quick to get behind Froome. The man who has been claimed by Kenya, South Africa and Britain was now even being claimed to some extent by Italy because of the time he spent there while riding for Barloworld.

'This is a new Cannibal that does not eat dirty,' was how one Italian newspaper responded to the doping allegations, alluding to the nickname of the legendary Eddy Merckx.

Questions were also bound to be asked of Froome's character. If he can hack into the Kenya Cycling Federation's account to log an entry in the 2006 under-23 World Time Trial Championships in Salzburg, can he dope? If he can hold onto a motorbike during the climb up the Mortirolo in the 2010 Giro d'Italia – for which he was disqualified – can he dope? (In Froome's defence in the case of the motorbike incident, he believed the tour was over for him because of an injury to his right knee, and he says he had already made the decision to quit. 'I was trying to get to the top,' he said of a race that was over for him.)

And during the 2013 Tour de France, Froome was penalised 20 seconds on stage 18 in the Alps for illegal feeding. Riders are allowed to replenish food and liquids during stages on the tour. But this must be done at designated feed zones. During the stage, and outside the feed zone, Froome 'bonked' – the cycling term for a sudden drop in blood sugar. Having missed an earlier opportunity to eat because of what he said were mechanical problems with the team vehicle, Froome asked Richie Porte to collect a power gel for him in the final 5 kilometres of the stage.

While later saying he was happy to accept the penalty, he did state that, 'technically it was actually Richie Porte who fed [me] from the car, and not myself. I fed from Richie Porte, so maybe that's something that needs to be taken into consideration.'

Porte was also penalised, but many cycling fans felt Froome was wrong to shift the blame to his loyal teammate.

Nevertheless, it was the very fact that Froome appeared physically vulnerable on this stage that, for many, proved that he was not doping. Says Tucker:

> I think it was good that he showed weakness on Alpe d'Huez and Semnoz. He tried to attack, and Nairo Quintana and Joaquim Rodriguez were able to stay with him and even counter-attack and drop him. Sure, by then he'd won the tour and maybe didn't quite have to dig so deep. But, if he'd ridden all four big climbs the same as he rode the first two, it would have been very difficult to make a case for him. Normal physiological behaviour cannot be that good so consistently.

And, of course, there will always be lingering questions surrounding Froome's sudden and unorthodox rise from *domestique* to grand-tour contender and Tour de France champion. As Tucker says, there are very few instances where a Chris Froome happens. Tennis is not a great example because it's a technical sport where you have to acquire the skill, but the likes of Rafael Nadal, Novak Djokovic and Roger Federer were identified when they were 14 or 15 years old. Everyone knew that these guys would one day be maybe not as good as they are, but they knew they were going to be in that top 20. It's the same in running. At 15, everyone said Usain Bolt was going to be a world champion. Carl Lewis was the same as a junior. When Haile Gebrselassie was 17 or 18, he won the world junior title, and everyone could see there's the next guy. So Froome hasn't followed the normal trajectory. But it doesn't mean that there can't be someone who does that. The bilharzia may well have affected him so much that he was 10 per cent off his capabilities. So it's not definitive, but it's the reason people ask the questions.

As Tucker admits, when it comes to cycling and doping, it's an argument as circular as the wheels of a bicycle. But, he concedes, it's an argument that has to go on. 'The sport of cycling had so much inertia. It was like this giant steamship going in one direction. Slowly people are nudging it in a different direction. But if people stop asking these questions it will just go back to course. It has to happen. I would like to believe in Chris Froome, and the other fact that gives me hope is that in the 2013 Tour de France, the whole Sky team didn't dominate. They looked human quite a few times.'

But the question most cycling fans are asking is, how can we be sure the riders are clean? And if not, what is the gap between the doping and the tests?

When working with Tyler Hamilton on his book, Daniel Coyle asked him the question, how could you avoid testing positive for all those years? He says Hamilton just laughed before telling him, 'The tests are easy to beat. We're way, way ahead of the tests. They've got their doctors, and we've got ours, and ours are better. Better paid, for sure. Besides, the UCI doesn't want to catch certain guys anyway. Why would they? It'd cost them money.' Hamilton also later said, 'If you were careful and paid attention, you could dope and be 99 per cent certain that you would not get caught.'

In defending himself against his accusers, Armstrong also famously stated, 'I have competed as an endurance athlete for 25 years with no spike in performance, passed more than 500 drug tests and never failed one.'

For Tucker and many others, the key to fighting doping in cycling lies in the success of the biological passport:

The biological passport closed the gap considerably. I remember, either one or two years ago the number of blood tests in the Tour de France was low. There were a lot of urine tests, but not a lot of bloods, which is not a good sign. The biological passport needs blood tests. But even the biological passport has its limitations in a new era in cycling where micro-doping is now the concern, namely lower levels of doping. Whereas before cyclists would be injecting large amounts of EPO every fourth day during a tour, micro-doping is a strategy of injecting smaller doses every day.

But, for the likes of Tucker, micro-doping is only a small dent in the anti-doping battle:

Doping deliverance?

As long as they're testing often and unpredictably then it's good because it changes behaviour. There's good evidence that as soon as they introduce a new test, the doping behaviour changes. Even Tyler Hamilton and Lance Armstrong admitted that as soon as the EPO test in the urine became available they had to go back to blood doping, and the dopers do it quickly.

Dopers behave fairly predictably, so, the more you squeeze and the more you scrutinise, the less they can dope. For example, five, ten or fifteen years ago, if you weren't doping, you couldn't win because doping gave you so much more. It didn't matter about your diet, training, psychology, equipment and everything you put together because it could never overcome the 10–15 per cent doping gave you. Now, with doping having been squeezed back, maybe it's 2 or 3 per cent. Without doping, you can now compete. That's the point. So the rider who is not doping, for the first time in a decade, has a chance. So I don't care too much that they're micro-doping. I hope they still get caught because it's still cheating. But it's not as bad as the situation where it's not possible to win the Tour de France without drugs. The only way you can stay ahead of the testing now is to dope less, as opposed to doping differently. The biological passport doesn't look for the substance, it looks for its effect. So, even if you got your doctor to give you something that's not on the market yet and is undetectable, if it caused the same effect as EPO you'd still get caught. So the idea of undetectable drugs wouldn't affect the passport's success. Unless it's a hormone that affects muscle recovery or something. But, for the blood, they're painted into a corner and the corner is getting smaller.

Tucker still watches cycling, but for the contest it produces. He is by no means convinced that the sport is clean of doping:

My conclusion from five years of studying the Tour de France is that I see enough to suggest that there is less doping by fewer riders. Is it clean? No. Is Froome dirty? Maybe, maybe not. Are the top-ten riders doping? There's a good chance that they are. But even if they are, it's less than they used to. I'm fairly optimistic that they're doping less, and fewer of them are doping. But there's definitely doping. Too little has changed. The people in charge are the same. The people who run the teams are the same. The doctors are the same. The sport directors are the same. You're not going to solve yesterday's problems with yesterday's people. It will take a generation or two. The leadership of the UCI needs to change. The team managements need to change. Cycling still hasn't reached that truth-and-reconciliation step. That's a big problem. Behavioural psychologists will tell you that people don't change their behaviour until they've disclosed their previous behaviour. There hasn't been full transparency, so how can we expect it to be different? There's definitely still doping.

But the doping is less, and I would still take that as a victory. It's a little bit sad, but it doesn't mean the game's over. Call it a battle won. The next stage will be to improve the biological passport, make the punishment harsher. It's just changing the incentive. The riders are rational. Can I dope? Yes. What are the chances of me getting caught? And how badly will I be punished if I'm caught? Make the punishment harsher, and you'll have less doping.

Ultimately, though, cycling's very nature as a team sport when it comes to the grand tours could remain its ultimate handicap in the fight against doping. In an individual sport, the athlete makes the decision to dope or not. Should he decide not to, his success is still determined by his ability to compete.

However, in cycling, it can be all or nothing. If you don't dope in a team or an environment that encourages this, you lose your job. Your place in the team is taken by somebody else who is willing to dope.

Lest we forget, professional cycling is all about money. Teams are run along the same lines as Formula 1 teams. There are numbers and targets that must be met. If you're not meeting them, you're out. There are sponsors to keep happy, and the way to do this is to win. This is a sport about making money.

* * *

So what of Chris Froome? At the time of his greatest triumph, he faces his greatest scrutiny. And so it should be. For the most part, he has handled it impeccably well. And this will be his role in the new era of cycling. Froome has stated that he wants to prove you can win the Tour de France riding clean. He has said that the code of *omertà* within the peloton has been broken, that other riders no longer tolerate doping of any form by their teammates or opponents. Froome is happy to lead a new breed of professional cyclists and take upon himself the mantle of the moral compass for the sport. As such, he should be happy to face the questions as well – however constant they are, however irritating they are.

'At the moment, everyone's going to question, as they should. The scrutiny is a good thing, and Froome should welcome it too. I can understand why he gets upset. But I would say within three to five years, given the scrutiny in cycling, something would come out if there was doping. Something would stick a little bit more,' says Tucker.

At the end of 3 404 kilometres of questions and allegations, Chris Froome made his last case for the defence when he rode into Paris as the Tour de France champion: 'In a way, I'm glad that I've had to face those questions, that after all the revelations last year and just the tarnished history over the last decade, all that's been channelled toward me now. I feel I've been able to deal with it reasonably well throughout this tour, and hopefully that's sent a strong message to the cycling world that the sport has changed – and it really has. The peloton's standing together, the riders are united and it's not going to be accepted any more.'

The question arises that we may look back one day and admonish ourselves for not having recognised Chris Froome's 2013 Tour de France for the genuine greatness it entailed. Had we all failed to truly appreciate one of the greatest clean performances in cycling because we were so fixated on the negatives of the past? As fans, had we missed the opportunity to truly appreciate the dawn of a new age in cycling? One where Bradley Wiggins and Chris Froome proved to us that the body was capable of racing clean, one where they were ushering in a new era of not winning at all costs – a major cultural shift in a sport tainted from the very start of its existence – Wiggins and Froome making history as the riders winning the Tour de France clean.

As scientists, had we not appreciated the opportunity to see just how far a clean rider could push himself in the hardest race of all? To establish new limits, asking new questions of just how much punishment the body can take to stay at the top level. Can a rider win multiple Tours de France riding clean, or is it just not possible to win more than one, perhaps two, because of the physical toll it takes on the body?

Froome is a patient man, so, while not entirely happy with not having his talent immediately recognised now for what it is, he is content to let time be the judge on this one. 'This is one yellow jersey that will stand the test of time,' he told the world as he stood on the podium in Paris. That will go down as one of the most powerful statements in the history of cycling. And, ultimately, history will tell if Froome is right.

'It always does,' says Tucker, who will be watching from his computer screen.

References

Chapter 1

Alasdair Fotheringham, 'Bradley Wiggins: "Tom will be watching over me on Ventoux"', *The Independent*, 25 July 2009, http://www.independent.co.uk/sport/general/others/bradley-wiggins-tom-will-be-watching-over-me-on-ventoux-1760541.html (accessed 15 October 2013).

James Bennett, 'Fans and cycling legends alike discuss Mont Ventoux in Tour's centenary year', ABC News, *The World Today*, 15 July 2013, http://www.abc.net.au/worldtoday/content/2013/s3803336.htm (accessed 14 October 2013).

Dan Seaton, 'Mont Ventoux asks the same thing of winners and losers: everything', *VeloNews*, 14 July 2013, http://velonews.competitor.com/2013/07/news/mont-ventoux-asks-the-same-thing-of-winners-and-losers-everything_295182 (accessed 14 October 2013).

Alasdair Fotheringham, 'Tour de France 2013: Historic climb on Mont Ventoux gives us Chris Froome with a view', *The Independent*, 14 July 2013, http://www.independent.co.uk/sport/cycling/tour-de-france-2013-historic-climb-on-mont-ventoux-gives-us-chris-froome-with-a-view-8708080.html (accessed 15 October 2013).

Nick Westby, 'Froome's Ventoux heroics leave us desperate for repeat performance', *Yorkshire Post*, 24 July 2013, http://www.yorkshirepost.co.uk/sport/other-sports/cycling/froome-s-ventoux-heroics-leave-us-desperate-for-repeat-performance-1-5885092 (accessed 15 October 2013).

References

Chapter 2

'Why do Kenyans dominate marathons?', *BBC News*, 3 November 2005, http://news.bbc.co.uk/2/hi/africa/4405082.stm (accessed 15 October 2013).

John Franklin Hay, 'Joseph's Ride', 14 June 2012, Bike Kenya blogspot, http://bikekenya2012.blogspot.com/ (accessed 14 October 2013).

Tim Noakes, *Lore of Running*, Human Kinetics, 1986: 406.

Ibid.: 448.

Chapter 3

Lourensa Eckard, '*Voorste Tour-ryer voel tuisste in SA*', *Beeld*, 17 July 2013, http://www.beeld.com/nuus/2013-07-17-voorste-tour-ryer-voel-tuisste-in-sa (accessed 16 October 2013).

Carryn-Ann Nel, '*Fietstoer se no. 1 word in SA groot*', *Beeld*, 16 July 2013, http://www.beeld.com/nuus/2013-07-16-fietstoer-se-no-1-word-in-sa-groot (accessed 16 October 2013).

Simon Burnton, 'No shortcuts to Tour de France for quietly determined Chris Froome', *Guardian*, 19 July 2013, http://www.theguardian.com/sport/2013/jul/19/tour-de-france-chris-froome (accessed 15 October 2013).

Ibid.

Ibid.

Ibid.

Mike Finch, 'EXCLUSIVE: Chris Froome − Top of the world', *Bicycling*, 22 February 2013, http://www.bicycling.co.za/news-people/chris-froome-top-of-the-world/ (accessed 15 October 2013).

Andrew Hood, 'The story of Brailsford's Froome discovery dates back to 2006', *VeloNews*, 10 July 2013, http://velonews. competitor.com/2013/07/news/the-story-of-brailsfords- froome-discovery-dates-back-to-2006_294574 (accessed 16 October 2013).

'Why Kenya lost star rider Froome', Capital FM, 22 July 2013, http://www.capitalfm.co.ke/sports/2013/07/22/why-kenya- lost-star-rider-froome/ (accessed 16 October 2013).

'The big interview: Chris Froome', *Cycling Weekly*, 3 June 2008, http://www.cyclingweekly.co.uk/news/latest/346898/the-big- interview-chris-froome.html (accessed 16 October 2013).

Jean-François Quénet, 'Tough start to Froome's first Tour', *Cyclingnews*, 7 July 2008, http://www.cyclingnews.com/news/ tough-start-to-froomes-first-tour (accessed 15 October 2013).

Chapter 4

Kevin McCallum, 'Froome goes from St John's to Sky', IOL Sport 28 June 2013, http://www.iol.co.za/sport/cycling/froome- goes-from-st-john-s-to-sky-1.1538918#.Ulzt3ySiRq4 (accessed 16 October 2013).

Greg LeMond, 'Cobblestones, crashes and potential winners of the Tour', *Cyclingnews*, 9 July 2010, http://www.cyclingnews. com/blogs/greg-lemond/cobblestones-crashes-and-potential- winners-of-the-tour (accessed 16 October 2013).

Tyler Hamilton & Daniel Coyle, *The Secret Race – Inside the Hidden World of the Tour de France: Doping Cover-ups and Winning at All Costs*, Bantam Books, 2012: 40.

'Froome – A product of the WCC', Union Cycliste Internationale, 23 July 2013, http://www.uci.ch/Modules/ENews/

References

ENewsDetails.asp?id=OTQ1Mw&MenuId=MTI2Mjc (accessed 16 October 2013).

Matthew Magri, '"Phenomenon Froome" discovery made in Bergamo', *Corriere della Sera*, 17 July 2012, http://translate. google.co.za/translate?hl=en&sl=it&u=http://bergamo. corriere.it/bergamo/notizie/sport/12_luglio_17/froome-tour-france-corti-ciclismo-curno-2011039641483.shtml&prev=/ search%3Fq%3D (accessed 15 October 2013).

Andrew Hood, 'Chris Froome: Out of Africa and onto the Vuelta podium', *VeloNews*, 15 September 2011, http://velonews. competitor.com/2011/09/news/chris-froome-out-of-africa-and-onto-the-vuelta-podium_192373 (accessed 15 October 2013).

Gregor Brown, 'Froome taking great strides', *Cyclingnews*, 21 November 2008, http://www.cyclingnews.com/news/froome-taking-great-strides (accessed 16 October 2013).

Laurent Fignon, *We Were Young and Carefree*, Yellow Jersey Press, 2009: 88.

Chris Sidwells, 'Froome could win this Tour de France', The Roar, 4 July 2012, http://www.theroar.com.au/2012/07/04/ chris-froome-could-win-this-tour-de-france/ (accessed 15 October 2013).

James Callow, 'Britain's Chris Froome takes shock lead of Vuelta a España', *Guardian*, 29 August 2011, http://www. theguardian.com/sport/2011/aug/29/chris-froome-bradley-wiggins-vuelta (accessed 16 October 2013).

Ian Chadband, 'Tour de France 2013: The incredible rise of Chris Froome – and how he was almost killed by a hippo', *The Telegraph*, 27 June 2013, http://www.telegraph.co.uk/sport/ othersports/cycling/tour-de-france/10144509/Tour-de-France-2013-the-incredible-rise-of-Chris-Froome-and-how-he-was-almost-killed-by-a-hippo.html (accessed 16 October 2013).

Andrew Hood, 'Still living with bilharzia parasite, Froome says he has no drug exemptions', *VeloNews*, 16 July 2013, http://velonews.competitor.com/2013/07/news/froome-confirms-no-tue-still-treated-for-bilharzia-parasite_295548 (accessed 15 October 2013).

Ibid.

'Froome set for California', Sky Sports, 14 May 2011, http://www1.skysports.com/cycling/news/17565/6930307/Froome-set-for-California (accessed 15 October 2013).

James Startt, 'Team Sky's Christopher Froome is the Tour de France's most surprising rider', *Bicyling*, 16 July 2012, http://www.bicycling.com/news/2012-tour-de-france/tour-features/team-skys-christopher-froome-tour-de-frances-most-surprising-rider (accessed 16 October 2013).

'Froome ready for action', TeamSky.com, 17 August 2011, http://www.teamsky.com/article/0,27290,17546_7107529,00.html (accessed 16 October 2013).

Chapter 5

Bradley Wiggins, *My Time*, Yellow Jersey Press, 2012: 70.

Giles Whittell, 'Chris Froome: Cycling's next superstar', *The Times*, 29 June 2013, http://www.thetimes.co.uk/tto/magazine/article3799206.ece (accessed 20 October 2013).

Sean Yates, *It's All About the Bike*, Transworld Publishers, 2013.

Bradley Wiggins, *My Time*: 209.

Giles Whittell, 'Chris Froome: Cycling's next superstar'.

References

Chapter 6

http://stevetilford.com/2013/07/15/its-all-about-froome/ (accessed 19 October 2013).

http://veloclinic.tumblr.com/post/54770388624/tour-de-france-2013-stage-8-dpvam-ax3-warning-shot (accessed 20 October 2013).

Tyler Hamilton & Daniel Coyle, *The Secret Race*: 51.

Ibid.: 137.

Ibid.: 81.

http://www.theguardian.com/sport/2013/jul/18/team-sky-chris-froome-data (accessed 20 October 2013).

William Fotheringham, 'Tour de France 2012: Bradley Wiggins retains race leader's jersey', *Guardian*, 8 July 2012, http://www.theguardian.com/sport/2012/jul/08/tour-de-france-bradley-wiggins-yellow-jersey (accessed 20 October 2013).

http://www.theguardian.com/sport/blog/2012/jul/13/bradley-wiggins-dope-drugs (accessed 19 October 2013).

Bradley Wiggins, *My Time*: 190.

Tyler Hamilton & Daniel Coyle, *The Secret Race*: 19.

Richard Moore, 'Froome finishes rough road to Paris with hope for the journey ahead', *Guardian*, 28 July 2008, http://www.theguardian.com/sport/2008/jul/28/cycling.tourdefrance (accessed 20 October 2013).

Daniel Benson, 'Froome shocked on doping in team', *Cyclingnews*, 28 July 2008, http://www.cyclingnews.com/news/froome-shocked-on-doping-in-team (accessed 19 October 2013).

Bike Pure, http://bikepure.org/2013/06/transparency-grand-tour-contenders/ (accessed 19 October 2013).

Ibid.

'Tour de France: Scot David Millar defends Chris Froome over doping questions', *Daily Record*, 8 July 2013, http://www. dailyrecord.co.uk/sport/other-sports/cycling/tour-de-france-scot-david-2037711 (accessed 20 October 2013).

Tom McGowan & Amanda Davies, CNN, http://edition.cnn. com/2013/07/09/sport/david-millar-tour-de-france-doping-cycling/index.html (accessed 20 October 2013).

Ibid.

Ibid.

John Stevenson, 'Team Sky principal Sir Dave Brailsford admits using Belgian doctor Geert Leinders was a "mistake"', 9 July 2013, http://road.cc/content/news/87579-team-sky-principal-sir-dave-brailsford-admits-using-belgian-doctor-geert-leinders (accessed 19 October 2013).

The Irish Times, http://www.irishtimes.com/sport/second-captains (accessed 19 October 2013).

Jeff MacGregor, 'The Age of Innocence', 24 July 2013, http://espn. go.com/espn/story/_/id/9502826/chris-froome-chris-davis-doping-questions?src=mobile (accessed 20 October 2013).

Tyler Hamilton & Daniel Coyle, *The Secret Race*: 24.

Bibliography

Giles Belbin, 2013. *Mountain Kings: Agony and Euphoria on the Peaks of the Tour de France.* Punk Publishing

Jean Bobet, 2008. *Tomorrow, We Ride.* Mousehold Press

Lucy Fallon and Adrian Bell, 2005. *Viva La Vuelta! – The Story of Spain's Great Bike Race.* Mousehold Press

Laurent Fignon, 2009. *We Were Young and Carefree.* Yellow Jersey Press

William Fotheringham, 2003. *Put Me Back on My Bike: In Search of Tom Simpson.* Random House

Tyler Hamilton & Daniel Coyle, 2012. *The Secret Race – Inside the Hidden World of the Tour de France: Doping Cover-ups and Winning at All Costs.* Bantam Books

Tim Noakes, 1986. *Lore of Running.* Human Kinetics

Bradley Wiggins, 2012. *My Time.* Yellow Jersey Press

Sean Yates, 2013. *It's All About the Bike.* Transworld Publishers

Acknowledgements

In any team, it's those around you who make you look good.

To my wife, Ursula, and my boys, Jack and Ethan, thank you so much for your unending support, encouragement, patience and enthusiasm while I was working on the book. You give meaning to all of this.

To Jeremy Boraine, Eugene Ashton and Ceri Prenter of Jonathan Ball Publishers, and Mark Ronan, thank you for your faith and for helping to make this book better with your invaluable input.

My thanks also go to John Bridger, Roger Cameron, Alex Carera, Gavin Cocks, Gareth Edwards, Andrew Hood, Robbie Hunter, David Kinjah, Alan Lion-Cachet, Kevin McCallum, Andrew McLean, Charles Mose, Karel Mouton, Jon Patricios, Steve Tilford, Ross Tucker and Toni Williams, for giving so generously of your time to tell me your stories and take me into the fascinating world of the professional peloton.

Michael Vlismas
Somerset West
October 2013